MULTIDIMENSIONAL EVOLUTION

Kim McCaul's experiential account of life beyond the physical dimension carries a challenge that cannot be ignored, namely, by what mechanism of mind and body can such extraordinary experiences be explained? As an anthropologist, McCaul is well aware of the standard academic explanations for such curious psychic events, but when non-standard experiences erupt frequently in one's own daily life, and are intelligently attested to by others, then perhaps the standard explanations require some adjustment. McCaul's careful, methodical and questioning approach is therefore to be applauded, for in the face of experiences that often transcended normal categories of experience altogether, he held his nerve.

Douglas Lockhart, author of *Going Beyond the Jesus Story* and *The Mar Saba Codex*

Multidimensional Evolution

Personal Explorations
of Consciousness

Multidimensional Evolution

Personal Explorations
of Consciousness

Kim McCaul

Winchester, UK
Washington, USA

First published by Sixth Books, 2013
Sixth Books is an imprint of John Hunt Publishing Ltd., Laurel House, Station Approach,
Alresford, Hants, SO24 9JH, UK
office1@jhpbooks.net
www.johnhuntpublishing.com
www.6th-books.com

For distributor details and how to order please visit the 'Ordering' section on our website.

Text copyright: Kim McCaul 2013

ISBN: 978 1 78279 088 4

A CIP catalogue record for this book is available from the British Library.

Design: Stuart Davies

Printed in the USA by Edwards Brothers Malloy

Disclaimer

The views expressed in this book are those of the author. They are not made on

behalf of and do not purport to represent the International Academy of

Consciousness, the International Institute of Projectiology and Conscientiology,

or any of the individuals named in the book.

Copyright Acknowledgment

A version of the account of the author's projection in the mentalsoma
on pages 160–163 was originally published in the *Journal of Conscientiology*, 2002,
Vol. 5, Issue 17.

We operate a distinctive and ethical publishing philosophy in all
areas of our business, from our global network of authors to
production and worldwide distribution.

CONTENTS

Acknowledgments

Douglas Lockhart commented generously on early drafts of this book and gave encouragement and valuable advice on the publication process. Sandie Gustus provided equally generous encouragement and advice on how to move my manuscript to publication and beyond. Many years ago Sandra Rodrigues heard only one of the stories that have ended up in this book and her insistence that it should be told provided an early incentive to pursue this project. Mike Lydon's inspiration to organize the '30-day writing challenge' created the perfect space to move the book along. Doreen Zeitvogel provided extremely careful, detailed and intuitive editorial input and in the final stretch of writing Antonio Pitaguari made valuable technical comments while Grace Love helped maintain a sense of urgency by checking at every opportunity whether I'd finished yet.

My beautiful wife Joanne provided consistent support, inspiration and constructive criticism, and our children Rory, Hope and Sinéad all play the important role of requiring me to keep things real simply by being in my life.

Deep gratitude goes to the three intraphysical protagonists without whom I would not be telling this story: Pak Suyono, Leia and Waldo Vieira. Their commitment to the evolution of all those they meet is what makes this story worth telling. Finally, I extend my deepest appreciation to the extraphysical helpers who have tirelessly and generously supported and shown great patience to this particular intraphysical team member!

PART 1

ABOUT THE BOOK

Chapter 1

Introduction

Definition:

Multidimensional evolution. The perpetual growth of an individual consciousness, across physical lifetimes and all other dimensions of manifestation, in personal maturity, sense of universalism, energetic control, and the ability to provide assistance to others.

We are all multidimensional beings, but most of us forget this most of the time. Many people spend entire lifetimes unaware of it, though some few are born fully aware of their multidimensional selves. Most of us who do develop a sense of our nature during our physical lifetime then face the challenge of regaining full awareness of ourselves, of manifesting more of who we really are within this physical dimension. Those of us who embark on this quest may at times benefit from the assistance of a teacher or mentor, someone who is more aware of multidimensionality than we are at that point in time. Ultimately, we will realize that the whole world is here to teach us, that it is potentially the perfect school with fully developed virtual reality technology! Sometimes, though, we may require more personalized assistance.

The Teachers

In my case, three individuals stand out who most helped me awaken to the multidimensional nature of life. On the face of it, these three were very different people. Pak Suyono was an old Indonesian man who ran a meditation center, known as Shanti Loka, in central Java. Although highly eclectic, Shanti Loka was strongly influenced by Hindu and Buddhist approaches to

2

consciousness. In many ways, it fit the classic picture of the spiritual path, with a wise Asian teacher offering slightly obscure but profoundly personal insights and mind-altering experiences.

Leia, my second teacher, was a 'walk-in'. This means that the consciousness that ultimately used the body and went by that name was not the same consciousness that had originally activated that body at birth. That original consciousness had left when the body was in its early thirties and had been replaced by a new consciousness for a particular purpose. Leia offered cups of tea and biscuits in her living room, had a strong link to alien consciousnesses, no link to any religion, and lived an incon-spicuous country and family life in rural England.

My third teacher, Waldo Vieira, is a prominent figure in Brazil, author of dozens of books and the originator of major new approaches to understanding consciousness. His ideas have inspired thousands of people across Brazil and around the world, and they have led to the creation of numerous not-for-profit research and educational organizations that seek to practice a new and practical way of understanding multidimen-sional consciousness.

Despite these apparent differences, all three embraced and encouraged critical thinking and personal experience as essential evolutionary tools; and despite the seeming differences in their spiritual backgrounds, all three shared the same multidimen-sional view of life along with the same commitment to helping others grow in their self-awareness and ability to achieve their life's purpose. This book is about these three teachers and the understandings of consciousness they taught and lived.

All three impacted me directly through their energies in profoundly transformative ways. To put it another way, they used their psychic powers to help bring my awareness to previ-ously unconscious areas of my life in order to shift and discard old patterns of thought and emotion. This was done through what could be described as beneficial multidimensional interventions. They also provided me with techniques and under-standings that have enabled me to continue these transforma-tions by myself. This book describes some of the personal experi-ences, at times dramatic and frightening, that were caused by those interventions.

Content and Approach

The experiences I describe represent a range of phenomena that I consider to be universal features of the spiritual journey, if not in one lifetime, then in another. At times, I wondered whether it might be better to write a more abstract 'textbook', partly because I had some resistance to exposing some of the naive blunders and foolish vanities that marked parts of my journey. But in the end, I decided that revealing relevant personal experiences was coherent with my position of 'guinea pig–researcher' of my own consciousness.

Being both the guinea pig, the thing researched, and the researcher exemplifies my vision of a future science of consciousness. In this approach, personal experience is not relegated to the status of subjective irrelevance or scientific nuisance but is central to our understanding and to the devel-opment of models of consciousness. In that sense, and perhaps because I am an anthropologist, I consider this book an attempt at an ethnography of my own consciousness. As such, it includes accounts of awesome and extraordinary experiences of consciousness as well as of my psychological and mental hang-ups, flaws and weaknesses. I hope this approach will make some of the ideas more tangible and allow you to understand how I came to embrace the explanatory models that I describe in the next chapter and in the final part of the book.

The main proposition of this book is that multidimensional life is a universal human experience. The only thing that varies is our awareness of this. There is nothing airy-fairy about being connected with one's multidimensional aspects. Leaving my physical body, being aware of non-physical life around me or being conscious of having lived many lifetimes does not free me from having to live a practical physical life right now. I work, I raise my children, and I have to make everyday practical decisions about what to eat and how to dress. But having this awareness does imbue life with purpose, possibility and the continuous opportunity for learning and growth.

Another basic premise of this book is that my own view on things must be informed by personal experience. Over the years, I have encountered many ideas on spiritual life, for example: a person's wealth is a reflection of their spiritual evolution; if you do bad things in this life you will come back as an animal; certain combinations of incense will remove negative spirits; only if you follow Jesus will you be saved from hell; only if you apply a certain combination of techniques will you achieve enlightenment; you can achieve enlightenment in this life and will never have to come back in physical form; and so on and so forth! Sometimes such ideas were perhaps informed by particular experiences people had, but at other times they were simply received from others. In either case they had become accepted as absolute truths. 'Truth' readily turns into dogma, which in turn stifles our freedom to think about our experiences, broaden our understanding and develop new frameworks. This can occur equally in matters of spirituality and science. The approach I am advocating in this book is to use personal experiences of multidimensionality to inform an intellectual framework that will help us develop our understanding of our nature more broadly. This means that we never deal in 'truths', but only ever in 'relative truths' that may need to be revised on the basis of new insights and understandings.

Making experience my benchmark also means that there are a lot of things I have to feel ambiguous about because I just don't know. God, or an ultimate Creator of all things, would fall into that category for me. My own understanding of the way thought precedes material creation allows for the logical possibility that there is an Original Thinker. I have also enjoyed ecstatic states of consciousness in which I 'knew' that all life across all galaxies and dimensions is connected and interdependent and that there are amazing designs that govern existence across all of creation. But does that in any way relate to the notion of God? I don't know. As far as I can see, there are numerous other possibilities to account for the amazing nature of creation, and the issue does not seem to matter to my immediate evolutionary process. For that, all that is required is my readiness to take on those aspects of myself that get between me and my sense of connection with multidimensional consciousness. And while I am aware of having received frequent assistance with that process from both physical and non-physical sources, I do not consider such assistance to have been divine intervention! So on some questions, I must live with ambiguity.

Then there are those things for which I personally have no experiential evidence, yet what experiential evidence I do have on related issues suggests that one approach may be a better working hypothesis than another. One such hypothesis is that we are all on a journey through innumerable physical lives that will eventually end when we no longer need to return to this dimension. Personally, I have no awareness of ever having met a consciousness that was so highly evolved that it was in its last life as a human being before permanently shifting dimensions. But I do have experiential insight into different consciousnesses having very different levels of energetic control and personal maturity. I have also had personal retrocognitions (memories of past lives) that have led me to fully accept the concept of reincarnation. Consequently, I can accept the logic of a model where consciousnesses gradually develop in maturity until they no longer have any need to experience life through the dense energetic dimension of the physical body. Aside from making logical sense, this understanding provides a viable context for the particular point that I am experiencing right here and now in my series of existences. Still, if I am ever confronted with experiences that undermine this model, then I will have to alter my point of view. This, to me, is the fusion of spirituality and science, if spirituality is understood as a life lived for the purpose of spirit (or what I generally call 'consciousness') rather than the material body; and if science is defined as a model of knowledge based on rigorous experimentation, questioning and openness to refutation. The extent of this fusion depends on our own intimate posture and approach to life.

I happily admit that some of the ideas I present might sound crazy, especially if you have never thought of yourself as a multi-dimensional being or perhaps if your approach has been largely channeled through some of the more conventional religious or esoteric schools of thought. Regardless of your background, I strongly encourage you to adopt the following principle in reading this book:

Don't believe anything! Experiment and have your own experiences.

Adopting this principle does not mean dismissing unusual ideas out of hand. That in itself is an instinctual reaction arising from beliefs. Instead, I encourage you to approach my account with an open, albeit always questioning mind. Breaking our own mental and experiential molds from time to time is important for our continuous growth, and it helps us to avoid becoming stuck in comfortable grooves. Once you have allowed yourself to engage with the ideas, you can evaluate and assess and make up your own mind. I myself do not necessarily accept all the ideas I am presenting. At different times, my teachers told me things that I do not have the ability to verify or fully understand at this stage, but I have included them because I find them interesting. Even though I do not necessarily fully accept them, I am open to them as possibilities.

How This Book Can Help

As well as information designed to help you understand your own evolutionary processes, this book includes some of the techniques for meditation and energetic development that I was taught along the way. My hope is that if you work with these techniques, you will also have the opportunity to reawaken or deepen your awareness of that subtle part of yourself that knows exactly why you are here in this lifetime; that looks upon all of life (including yourself and all the people in your life) with the utmost unconditional love; and that has set itself a personalized goal, the realization of which will equate to a successful life. I call this subtle part 'consciousness', and it is consciousness that is at the core of all of us.

I hope that some of the stories and experiences I am about to share will assist you in gaining a greater understanding of the reality beyond your physical body. This book does not seek to provide evidence or convince you of anything. It describes my experiences as I gradually made my own discoveries about who I really am, and it presents information given to me along the way that has helped me to develop my understanding of multidimensionality.

Over the years, I have met many who have had similar experiences to the ones I will describe, and many, like me, took a long time to understand what was happening to them or went through periods of thinking there was something wrong with them. If you are in that position, it is my hope that this book will help you to become more comfortable with your experience of multidimensionality and to embrace it as an integral aspect of yourself. It is my further hope that this book will assist you, the reader, to develop new working hypotheses, to question any form of received wisdom and to take steps towards a conscious multidimensional life.

Chapter 2

Multidimensionality: Terms and Concepts

As I write this book, I am a different person from the one who had the early experiences I am about to describe. When I first left for Shanti Loka in Indonesia, I knew nothing about the multidimensional nature of life. I had not thought much about life after death, out-of-body experiences, spirits interacting with humans, reincarnation and so on. I am now writing this having spent the past 18 years studying and experimenting with such phenomena, and I have adopted a particular framework and way of speaking about them that I find especially clear and helpful. This terminology comes from the discipline of conscientiology, a particular approach to exploring consciousness that I studied in Brazil with Dr. Waldo Vieira, the third of my teachers discussed in this book. I learned this terminology only later in my journey, but I have decided to adopt this way of speaking about multidimensional experiences right from the start in my writing. I explain each new term as I introduce it, but if you are ever unsure of the meaning of a word you can consult the glossary at the end of the book.

You may already have had experiences that have alerted you to your own multidimensional nature and you are reading this because you are trying to find out more about it. I also know, however, that sometimes our conscious minds are a bit behind. That was certainly my experience. I was having multidimensional experiences for a while but, in my day-to-day state of mind, did not appreciate this fact. If this is your case, you may not even be sure as to why you are interested in this book, and reading it may feel like jumping in at the deep end. In fact, for someone who is new to the subject, the experiences I talk about in the next chapter might seem like nothing more than dreams or hallucinations. As you read through the book though, I hope the ideas I am introducing will become increasingly clear, just as they did for me. After all, even as the person who was having the experiences, I spent some years questioning whether they were real or just fantasies. In very basic terms, I gradually came to understand that who we are is not confined to our physical bodies and that these bodies are only one way in which we manifest.

Energy

We have all experienced energies that transcend the limits of the body. You may have found yourself thinking, for instance, that some people 'feel nice' while others 'feel creepy'. Or you may have had the experience of coming to a place that feels welcoming and inviting while another makes your hair stand on end. What we are reacting to in those situations, often unconsciously, are energies emanating from people or created by people at different places. The Eastern traditions all speak of this energy, and there are various names for it in different languages, such as *Chi* in Chinese, *Qui* (or *Ki*) in Japanese, and *Prana* in Sanskrit. Conscientiology calls this energy **bioenergy**, the energy of life. For each of us, these energies form a 'body' that permeates and animates our physical bodies and is really a subtle extension of the physical body. In conscientiology this body is called our **energosoma**, for energo- (energy) plus soma (body). The energosoma is like an energetic double in the sense that it has the same shape as the physical body. It is not, however, an independent body in the sense that our consciousness would use it without the physical body. Rather, the two are intimately intertwined. The energosoma is targeted in many alternative healing modalities such as Reiki, Shiatsu, Acupuncture and Homeopathy.

Most people these days have heard of chakras. These form an important part of the energosoma, ensuring the circulation of energies throughout the whole energetic system. But the energosoma is much more than just the main chakras often described in the general literature. It is composed of thousands of small chakras connected by energetic channels traversing the entire body. The energosoma is of fundamental importance to life in this dimension, which is ultimately energetic, and its well-being is closely related to our physical well-being. The energosoma develops as we grow in our multidimensional awareness and self-expression. Its condition depends on a range of factors, including such physical aspects as diet, exercise and drug use, but it is also influenced to a significant extent by our mental and emotional habits. Fear, anger, love, compassion, mental focus and dispersion will all be reflected in the energetic body, and you can learn a lot about yourself and others as you learn to interpret energies.

When I first became aware of my own energies at Shanti Loka, my main realization was that they were blocked and very messy. Once I started developing an awareness of this, their condition improved, but I also became more susceptible to energetic influences from other people. I would pick up on other people's moods and emotions, and I found it difficult to spend a long time in crowded places. These days, looking after my energies is a basic part of my daily personal hygiene regime, and I will be explaining some very effective techniques that, if applied in your own life with some persistence, can help you maintain your energetic balance.

Out-of-Body Experiences (OBEs)

Beyond the subject of energy, I learned that we can actually leave our physical bodies during sleep and that these departures involve the same principle as the more permanent departure that happens at physical death. It took quite a bit longer to learn this than it did to understand energy, in the sense of actually knowing it through experience rather than just having an intellectual concept. My first very impactful out-of-body experience happened not long after my arrival at Shanti Loka and was literally a wake-up call. But it took several more years after that for me to accept at a deep level that these experiences were real and that they had an immense significance regarding our true nature.

There are a number of reasons for this delay between actually having the experience and gaining a solid understanding of its significance. One of them is the common confusion of dreams and out-of-body states. In the Western world, we are culturally conditioned to interpret any experience that occurs while our bodies are asleep as a dream, and for a long time I believed my out-of-body experiences to be very intense dreams. The two phenomena do in fact share many traits. Both often leave only fleeting memories that disappear very quickly after waking unless they are immediately recorded, and both can have strange aspects to them that make them seem utterly bizarre and unrealistic.

The main difference between the two is that dreams are intrapsychic experiences, that is, they are confined to our own minds, while out-of-body experiences are real external experiences involving other people and real places. There can be other significant distinctions. The classic out-of-body experience, with a conscious departure from the physical body, which is seen from above lying in bed, is clearly not a dream. Similarly, the detailed observations of physical events (sometimes subsequently confirmed) in the case of some near-death experiences, an extreme type of out-of-body experience, are not dreams. Nor are any experiences where we have full awareness of who we are and of the fact that our bodies are asleep while we are doing whatever it is we are doing.

But for most people most of the time, out-of-body experiences take place at a limited level of awareness. We do not have any perception of leaving our bodies or of returning to them, and we are only semi-conscious for some of the time while outside of them. We may be having real interactions with other people, both those who are also in an out-of-body state and those who currently do not have a physical body at all ('people who have died'). But we also add content from our own mental processes, which overlay these interactions and make them seem dreamlike and confused. Consequently, out-of-body experiences and the dimensions they give us access to are much less tangible than our experiences during our physical waking state. It often requires a series of fully conscious out-of-body states for us to deeply appreciate their reality and significance to our life.

Often the only evidence we have of our out-of-body experiences is gained by registering our energetic condition upon awakening and taking note of any alterations that occurred during sleep, as these reflect the very real energetic interactions we engage in while out of the body. Also, there is a range of energetic phenomena that often, though not always, occur prior to leaving our bodies. They can include feeling vibrations, a sense of expansion and tingling in our extremities, and they are often the last thing we perceive before losing consciousness and missing the actual out-of-body period. However, with persistence, we can bring awareness to those periods.

This book is based on the understanding, acquired over many years, that our deeper reality is found beyond the physical dimension. As consciousnesses in the physical body, both our ability to fully manifest all of who we are and our awareness are actually incredibly restricted by the dense energies of this dimension. Many of us, consciously or unconsciously, get very frustrated at the restrictions we experience here. But it is precisely this experience of restriction that makes the physical dimension such a good training ground, as we try to successfully pursue our particular purpose in this physical life. It is our effort in the face of this resistance that underpins our evolution.

Basic Terms

Before going further, I would like to introduce a few terms that I will be using when speaking about our possible experiences of consciousness. I realize that some of these will be unfamiliar at first, but I think you will find them easy to pick up. By the end of the book, I hope you will also find them helpful to think more clearly about multidimensional existence.

Intraphysical and extraphysical

The first set of terms is **intraphysical** and **extraphysical**. The term '*intra*physical' relates to everything associated with the physical dimension in which we experience ourselves most of the time while awake in our physical bodies. You and I are currently both *intraphysical consciousnesses*, as are all other beings with physical bodies; that is, we are consciousnesses who are having an intraphysical experience by way of the physical body we are currently animating. '*Extra*physical' relates to everything associated with any other dimension. When we are 'dead' or when we are having an out-of-body experience, we manifest in an extraphysical dimension. While there is only one intraphysical dimension, there are innumerable extraphysical dimensions. These dimensions are inhabited by an array of beings who do not, at present, have physical bodies. They are all *extraphysical consciousnesses*, meaning that they are beyond or outside of the physical dimension. From our human perspective, the term '*extraphysical consciousness*' most commonly refers to 'dead people' or 'spirits'. But there are in fact many extraphysical consciousnesses who do not have human form and may never have experienced human life.

The most frequent mental image many of us have of life beyond the physical body is that depicted in movies, which often involves people who continue in an existence after death that is parallel and close to the physical dimension. In mediumship, channeling, and other means by which physical people communicate with extraphysical people, it is most common for the extraphysical consciousnesses who come through to be from dimensions closely linked to the physical. The reason for this is that communication is easier from dimensions that are energetically more in tune with each other. The greater the 'distance' or variation in frequencies between dimensions, the more difficult communication becomes. For example, it is relatively easy for an extraphysical consciousness who is still attached to physical life and carries very dense energies to make itself known here, for instance by 'haunting'. On the other hand, a refined and subtle extraphysical consciousness who engages with this dimension from a perspective of pure love for all beings is much less readily perceived. So while it is true that there are many people with denser energies who are still attached to the physical condition, many more still have moved on to other dimensions, some only a little removed from our physical world, others increasingly so.

The reason people move to one dimension or another is found in their minds. Rather than thinking of dimensions as 'places', we can more accurately think of them as 'states of mind'. People who share like patterns of thought and emotion will draw together in communal dimensions. An analogy is radio waves. If we want to hear a certain program, we need to tune our radio to the right frequency. While we are tuned to that frequency, so are hundreds or thousands of other people. With the radio, we can easily change the channel and join another community of listeners tuned to a different frequency, but with our thoughts and emotions, the tuning does not happen so easily. They too emit a very real energetic frequency, and the majority of us are mostly set to one main channel. It may broadcast a range of programs that give the impression of diversity, but underlying it is a basic pattern. So when we finally leave this physical body for good we will find ourselves with others who generally share this pattern. One important purpose of the process of evolution I describe in this book is to provide us with greater freedom in terms of the frequencies we can choose for our own minds.

Different types of bodies

The next set of terms I want to introduce is used to describe our *bodies of manifestation*: the **psychosoma, mentalsoma** and **energosoma**. Together with our **soma**, the physical body, these vehicles represent the full set of our bodies that together can be referred to as our **holosoma** (holo = complete + soma = body). When I say 'our bodies' I don't mean 'our' as in Kim's bodies and (insert your name)'s bodies. Our current names are themselves just tags for the densest of our bodies, the physical body or soma. This is the body we use to manifest here in the intraphysical dimension, while we use the psychosoma and mentalsoma to manifest in the extraphysical dimensions. When thinking about our bodies of manifestation, it is important to reflect on who it is that is manifesting through these bodies. When we have experiences outside the body, we realize that we are not our physical bodies. Similarly, in some of our more expansive states, we realize that we are also not our emotions or even our thoughts. Eventually, we come to know ourselves as pure consciousness, beyond any of the bodies that we use as vehicles to access different dimensions of experience.

As physical beings, our awareness is largely dominated by our soma or physical body in which we find ourselves during our waking state. While much more subtle, the psychosoma and mentalsoma are nonetheless essential in our manifestation. The *psychosoma* refers to the vehicle through which we manifest most frequently in extraphysical dimensions, either between physical lives or during projections of consciousness. The psychosoma is commonly known as the astral body or, in esoteric literature, the spirit double. 'Psychosoma' literally translates as soul (psycho-) body (soma). In appearance, the psychosoma is a subtle replica of our current human body. But because it is not physical, it has many attributes that are quite different from those we normally expect from our physical body. For example, our psychosoma can fly, pass through matter and change shape.

The *mentalsoma* refers to the vehicle through which we manifest in the mental dimension. This is also an extraphysical dimension in the sense that it is beyond the physical, but it is also beyond any of the attributes that still define the extraphysical dimensions of the psychosoma, such as space, time and shape. We can project, that is, we can have an out-of-body experience through the mentalsoma just as we can through the psychosoma, although the experience is quite different. The mentalsoma is not shaped like our physical body. It is an orb or a point of consciousness, and if we consciously manifest through the mentalsoma, we will be experiencing profound states of transcendental consciousness, often very difficult to put into language. Terms such as samadhi, satori, cosmic consciousness or enlightenment are often used to express experiences in the mentalsoma.

Finally, there is the energetic body or *energosoma*, which I introduced earlier, constituted of *bioenergy*. Not only does it animate our physical bodies: it is also the intermediary between the physical body and the psychosoma. When we project outside of the physical body, the energosoma provides a link between that body and the psychosoma through what is known as the 'silver cord'. When the physical body dies, this energetic link between it and the extraphysical bodies is permanently broken.

This may all sound a bit abstract if you have not consciously experienced these bodies for yourself, but at least you will understand what I mean when I use the terms, and the techniques I provide in this book may assist you in accessing your own experiences.

Another point of clarification relates to a key experience I will be describing throughout the book. So far I have used the term 'out-of-body experience' when referring to those experiences in which people perceive themselves to be conscious yet outside or separate from the physical body. 'Out-of-body experience' (OBE) and 'astral projection' are terms commonly used in the literature discussing this phenomenon, but from now on, I will use the term **projection of consciousness** or just **projection** to describe these experiences. The reason for this is that, although important researchers of extraphysical phenomena, such as Robert Monroe, have used the term 'out-of-body experience', it has also been used in psychological and medical research with the connotation that it refers to some sort of mental trick or psychological dissociation in which the mind merely conjures up the experience of being outside the body. The term also implies that those experiencing these states always consciously perceive themselves as being outside of the physical body at the time, when that is not actually the case. In fact, people often project without having a full awareness of being outside their physical bodies. The term *projection of consciousness* is therefore used here to unambiguously identify the fact that the consciousness is projecting itself from one dimension, in this case the intraphysical dimension, to another, the extraphysical dimension in a subtle body of manifestation.

Existential seriality

The final set of terms I want to introduce at this point relates to **existential seriality**, that is, the series of existences commonly known as the cycle of reincarnation. I discovered early on in my own journey the very real impact that past existences have on the present one. Some key concepts for this topic are: **desoma, resoma, intermissive period** and **self-mimicry**.

Desoma stands for 'deactivation of the soma' (remember that *soma* means body). This is commonly known as 'death'. The term 'death' is, however, profoundly misleading because it implies the end or extinguishment of the person when it is really only the body that is switched off. That is why the term 'desoma' is more accurate, because it emphasizes the transitional, non-final aspect of the process, which sees the consciousness leaving its previous physical vehicle for the last time and assuming a new stage of life in the extraphysical dimensions. *Resoma* refers to the 'reactivation of the soma', commonly known as 'birth', although strictly speaking reactivation occurs at the point of conception. This is the moment where we reconnect with matter after an intermissive period in the extraphysical dimensions, and our energies, together with our mother's, power the physical construction of the new body.

The *intermissive period* is the extraphysical period after desoma and before resoma. It is the life between lives! The intermissive period can be spent in many ways. Ideally, we become lucid not long after our desoma and return to our extraphysical origin, or home dimension. Here we are reunited with many old friends and feel truly at home. We can reflect on our last intraphysical period, on whether we achieved all we had hoped for and, if not, what aspects within us stopped us. Eventually, we prepare ourselves for the next resoma. We might take an *intermissive course* to prepare ourselves for the next life. Such intermissive courses can take many forms and include prestudying topics that we plan to use in our future careers or personal lives, but they can also deal with many different aspects of the multidimensional evolution of consciousness. Examples include the relationship between different dimensions, the mastery of energies, living with psychic perceptions, the projection of consciousness, providing assistance to other consciousnesses, and so on. It may be beneficial to think about whether you have participated in such an intermissive course, because if you have, you will have covered specific topics relevant to your current life. You might find that you are able to access ideas from that period that will help you move more decisively in the direction you set for yourself before you were born.

Not all of us return to our extraphysical origin after our desoma. Many of us never really become conscious of the fact that we no longer have a physical body. If we are in that category, we continue to act as if we did have such a body: we sleep, eat, walk and talk, and we neither fly nor use telepathy. People in that category also eventually have a resoma, but they do not participate in any intermissive courses, and their lives are much more instinctive and driven by karmic impulses.

Finally, *self-mimicry* is the experience of repeating actions, behaviors, thoughts and attitudes from past lives. You may well be familiar with self-mimicry from your current everyday existence. You may know, for example, that you have a tendency to react to your colleague, spouse or child in a way that is not conducive to a good interaction. Part of you does not want to react that way, yet before you know it, you have done it again. Or you always seem to find yourself in the same relationship patterns, the same kinds of jobs or even the same conversations. Again, you may have particular habits and addictive behaviors that you just can't seem to shake. That is all self-mimicry on the microcosmic scale. Now imagine this happening over lifetimes! Evolution means breaking old patterns and building new ones that open doors through which we have not yet passed. All the big shifts that happened for me in this lifetime resulted from becoming aware of patterns of self-mimicry and, from that realization, starting to chart new courses of action and thinking.

PART 2

CRACKING THE EGG

Chapter 3

Shanti Loka

Pak Suyono,
After our meditation last night, I felt as though something had been set loose inside me. As I said, I felt as though you had 'touched' a hidden part of me. I felt very fragile and lay down to feel the process. What I felt was something freeing itself from the middle section of my spine and trying to exit through the mouth. Could you help me understand this process? Thank you!

Answer:
Not subconscious. From another incarnation. Dabbling in occult forces. Negative purpose. Using elementals.

For as long as I could remember, the idea of past lives seemed quite reasonable to me, but I never really stopped to think much about it. After all, what concern was it to me in my life right now?

In 1995, I traveled to Indonesia to spend some time in a meditation center called Shanti Loka. In the weeks before leaving, I had done a doodle in my journal. It was of a baby bird, still in its egg but starting to peck away at the inside in an effort to hatch. It was a most rudimentary drawing, yet I was fascinated by the concept. How did the baby bird know to crack its protective shell and poke its head out? I had no idea where the inspiration for this drawing had come from, and I did not associate it with the trip I was about to take. I did not realize that I myself was about to hatch into a completely new perspective of the world.

But while my unconscious was sending me messages, at a conscious level I really wasn't sure why I was going. After spending several years 'partying' and traveling, the twelve months prior to this trip had seen a drastic change in my life. I had started at university and seemed to be doing all right academically. I had quit smoking cannabis and greatly reduced my alcohol consumption, and this had gone some way towards quieting the demons that had been plaguing my mind for the past few years. I had also spent much of the past year commuting between Kent in England, where I was studying, and Paris where I was going out with a beautiful French dancer. So what more could a young man want? Why did I feel so compelled to take this trip to an unknown meditation center?

Still, at some level beneath my mental chatter, I did know that the trip to Indonesia was somehow necessary, even urgent, yet I continued to deny this feeling the entire way there. Even on the plane to Jakarta, I was still planning an alternative tourist route that would take me to Sumatra, where I saw myself having a far more adventurous time than some meditation center could possibly offer. Or so I thought!

Once in Java, there were no more questions. I seemed to have entered a current that was propelling me along at its own volition, and after one or two nights in Jakarta, I was on a train heading south. After another couple of nights, I found myself in the city of Solo (Surakarta), the home of Shanti Loka.

Shanti Loka was run by Ananda Suyono, usually known as Pak (Mr.) Suyono. The center was aimed primarily at Westerners. Pak Suyono spoke fluent English, and that was the language in which all the sessions were conducted. I don't know much about Pak Suyono. During my one stay there, I was too overwhelmed with what was happening to me to find out much about him. I know that as a young man he spent some time studying yoga in India and received his name Ananda (Sanskrit for 'bliss') from his teacher. I understood he had inherited the house that served as his ashram from his parents. I don't know what he did when he was younger or even how long he had been running Shanti Loka. At the time of my stay, he seemed to be in his sixties or early seventies. He was tall and energetic with a full head of grey hair and a clean-shaven, unlined face.

Shanti Loka was an eclectic place. A large Buddha statue dominated the meditation room, but neither Buddhism nor any other established religion or philosophy was singled out at the center. Rather, Shanti Loka had its own philosophy which was summed up by a large letter 'B' that hung above Pak Suyono's chair in the meditation center.

'Be'
'Be what?'
'Be aware.'
'Be aware of what?'
'Be aware of your body.'
'Be, Be, Be!'

This was how Pak Suyono introduced the center's philosophy to new arrivals.

It was certainly not a large ashram. During my visit, there would be six to twelve foreigners staying at Shanti Loka at any one time, with people regularly leaving and arriving. I recall one person who had been there for almost a year. Some were there for their second or third visit, while others came for a few days and then left again. Occasionally, a few locals would join in the evening meditation sessions.

The program was quite simple. Every weeknight, people staying at the center were expected to attend a session that started at 7 p.m. and ran until somewhere between 8 and 9:30 p.m. The rest of the day and all weekends were completely free, and many of us would go on trips to surrounding attractions such as the ancient temples at Borobodur and Prambanan for weekends.

During the evening sessions, residents were encouraged to relate their daily experiences. Pak Suyono asked us to be mindful of two phases in our lives while at Shanti Loka. One phase was the brief period in which we practiced the 'introspective meditation' during the evening sessions. This involved Pak Suyono talking us through a process of body relaxation as outlined in detail below. The other phase was everything else we did in our daily life. This he referred to as 'daily meditation', a prompt for us to experience our daily life with the same awareness we brought to the meditation practice. Internal events that people perceived during their day-to-day experiences seemed just as important to Pak Suyono as some of the transcendental experiences people had during the meditation sessions.

It probably doesn't sound like much to be sitting in a room chatting and then spending some time sitting quietly, just being aware of our bodies. Yet I have no doubt that everybody who spent a somewhat longer time at Shanti Loka (I spent a mere five weeks, others spent many months) came away changed. To my own surprise, I took to the whole meditation business like a fish to water. It wasn't something I had previously ever done, but as soon as I was introduced to it, meditation became a very important and natural part of my life.

For the first two or three weeks, I enjoyed feeling calm and contemplative. Then the event occurred that I alluded to at the outset of this chapter. The people staying at Shanti Loka could write down any questions they might have about their experiences. Pak Suyono would take the questions away overnight and hand the notes back with an answer the following day. He said that the answers were communicated to him during the night. I don't think he ever explained by whom, but even then I assumed it to be by one or more extraphysical consciousnesses. Or it may have been that Pak Suyono had psychic abilities (i.e. the ability to gain information about people or events by psychic means) that gave him intimate insight into people, but that he did not want to take credit for the answers. He certainly took a number of actions to make sure students did not idolize him. For example, unlike conventional gurus, he would advise people *not* to think of him when they felt in need of spiritual help or energy after they had left the ashram. Rather, they should think of Shanti Loka itself, because according to Pak Suyono, it was the place that was the source of the beneficial energy we were experiencing there, not him. Pak Suyono once said that the era of gurus was coming to an end, and I understood him to be saying that people needed to take responsibility for their own spiritual development and not seek to 'outsource' it to an external 'master'.

The note quoted at the outset of this chapter arose from an experience during one of the evening sessions. I was happily talking about some experiences that had occurred during the day and that to me seemed to represent new levels of awareness. Pak Suyono appeared quite disinterested and merely replied, 'You've got to go deeper.' As he said those words, I felt as if he, or rather his energy, touched my very core. I felt shaken, and once the session ended, I did not accompany the others on the usual dinner outing but withdrew to my room, where I was overwhelmed by the sensation of something unpleasant wanting to be released from within myself. This something seemed to detach itself from my spine and push its way up through my mouth. It wasn't a physical thing: it was energy, but it felt very real and I wretched as if I was going to vomit. I was fearful and confused. Following that incident, I became emotionally fragile and in some ways quite neurotic.

I became hypersensitive to energies in general. I would feel the emotional energies of other people in my body and mind and find it a challenge to be in crowded places. I suddenly became very aware that meat really was the flesh of dead animals, and I oscillated between states of profound peace during 'introspective meditation' and states of confusion that threatened to overwhelm me during my 'daily meditation'. My mind was clearly going through some major readjustments, and this was evidenced for me by the fact that I was almost incapable of reading anything during this period. Shanti Loka had a substantial library of esoteric and religious books, but in numerous attempts to read, I found myself incapable of taking anything in, repeatedly rereading single pages until finally giving up. External knowledge was not what I needed at the time.

These days, I look back at that period and see it as an opening of myself to extraphysical dimensions, a partial lifting of the veil, as it were, that resulted in an evolutionary crisis and the beginning of a healing process that would have a number of further installments. But at the time, I just felt like I was going crazy. On a couple of occasions, while walking through the streets of Solo, I would freeze at the sight of some plastic bags being blown across the road. To any other observer they were merely empty plastic bags, carelessly discarded and left to the whims of the wind. But it took me some time to be sure that they were not ferocious dogs on the loose and coming for me. These were brief but very unpleasant moments until my will finally succeeded in fighting off the urge to run away from these plastic bags.

Another impactful experience at Shanti Loka was, quite literally, a wake-up call. One morning I was in the liminal stage between waking and sleeping. I had always enjoyed that stage and liked rolling over for another sleep, as the morning sleeps usually provided memorable dreams. This morning I was about to turn around when I noticed a presence next to my bed. Somehow in my drowsiness this did not really register as odd, and when the presence clearly told me to get up, I replied, 'In a minute.' I was about to turn over again, when the person kicked me in the head. I flew up, now fully awake, crying, 'OK, OK!' to whoever had woken me so roughly. There was nobody there. The kick to the head had been an extraphysical one, and I had perceived it while in my psychosoma. But it certainly woke me up. From then on I tended to start the day by jumping out of bed as soon as I first awoke, making sure I did not receive another kick. The message conveyed in that simple intervention was that I had spent the last 24 years sleeping and that it was now time to wake up and get on with real living. Only five years and two children later did I venture to stay in bed in the morning if I ever had the chance, but even now I still feel the urge to make this time productive by trying to take my mental awareness into the sleep state.

I think it was these kinds of multidimensional interventions that were behind much of the transformation that happened at Shanti Loka. The meditation technique itself made people receptive to such assistance. It got their energetic bodies moving, quieted their minds and predisposed them to multidimensional experiences. The technique was really quite simple. We would all sit upright on our chairs, uncross our arms and legs, and close our eyes. Then Pak Suyono would talk us through our bodies:

Be aware of the process of relaxation in your feet … be aware of your feet … your feet.

Be aware of the process of relaxation in your calves … be aware of your calves … your calves …

And so on through the knees, thighs, abdomen, chest, shoulders, arms and hands, neck and head. We would keep our focus on each area for perhaps a minute or so. Then, once he had gone through all the body parts, he would say:

Now become aware of the process of relaxation in your whole body … be aware of your whole body … your body …

And after a period of focusing our attention on the whole body, he would say:

And now let go …

At this point I would seek to let go of anything relating to my physical body and my sense of self as well as space, time and shape.

What happened when I started applying this technique seemed like magic at the time, but that was because I did not know much about the energetic constitution of the human body.

I became aware of parts of my body I had never been aware of before. I had clear perceptions of my organs and my muscles and sinews. I would hear distant sounds as if they were close by. And I became aware of a part of myself I hadn't even known existed: my energetic body. During one session, while being aware of the whole body, I could feel it deeply relaxed. But just beyond the body, I could feel something else, like a sheath, smooth and firm, surrounding my whole body. In another session, again while feeling my whole body, I felt like a patchwork person. One area buzzed with energy, while another felt hot, and still another depleted. In many sessions, I would feel intense pressure on my head, usually in the areas of the frontochakra (third eye) and the crown chakra (the area at the top of the head). Not that I knew about chakras at the time. I would also feel pressures in other parts of my body, and I would break into intense sweats and feel tingly all over, all as a result of sitting and being aware.

One day, as we were being aware of the process of relaxation in the abdomen, I experienced an energetic release that nearly knocked me out of my chair. I felt quite groggy after the meditation and told Pak Suyono of my experience. He asked me if I had ever done any martial arts involving the use of energies. I had! He quickly pointed out that martial arts were not always bad, but that you had to know what you were doing. I attribute the blocked energy in my abdomen to a brief period when I practiced kickboxing. As part of the training, we were taught certain techniques taken from Shaolin Kung Fu in which energy was pushed to and from the abdomen. We certainly weren't taught any of the finer details of this martial art, and it was basically treated as a means of allowing people to use the energy violently in kickboxing combat. Without knowing it, I had created a blockage through the misapplication of an energy technique.

What I came to appreciate through applying the Shanti Loka meditation over time was that such deliberate but unskillful manipulation of energies was not the only way that we create blockages. We all store energy in our bodies all the time. Every prolonged emotion or mental preoccupation results in an energetic reality stored in the body. There is no separation between the physical and subtler energies: physical injuries have energetic repercussions just as energetic blockages will manifest as physical conditions.

I persisted with the meditation practice after leaving Shanti Loka, and as I describe in the next chapter, it seemed to open up a continuous release of deeply stored energies linked to emotions and thoughts. The dynamic of this practice, of being deeply and intently aware and finally 'letting go', has come to exemplify an important aspect of the evolutionary dynamic to me. As humans, we continuously seek to identify ourselves to ourselves: 'I am ... 'dumb', 'intelligent', 'good-looking', 'fat', 'witty', 'powerful', 'hopeless', like this and like that. Such identifications run through our heads all the time, often unconsciously. As we grow in maturity and awareness, we learn to separate who we really are from these labels. We become aware, even if only in glimpses, that we are 'consciousness' (*atman*, Buddha mind, soul, divine principle or whatever word works for you), immortal and indefinable behind all the labels we attach to our current human form. To achieve this awareness, we need to first become aware, at ever deeper levels, of the labels that we impose, and then we need to let go of them; not fight or resist, but let go.

Of all the experiences I had during my stay at Shanti Loka, the ones described above were probably the most intense, but there were many others involving sensations of energies and changes in perception that together contributed to altering my appreciation of the world. Some might seem mundane, like the time a week or two after I arrived in Solo, when I looked up while walking along the street and noticed mountains on the horizon I had never noticed before. This was deeply symbolic to me of the state of unawareness in which I had moved about up to that time.

Others, I have since come to understand, were the result of the differing perceptions we have in the psychosoma. Like the times I would meditate lying down in the hall with my eyes closed yet was able to see physical people moving about the side of the room. I could not see them once I opened my eyes due to the angle of my head, but they were there, and I had seen them with the different vision we have in the psychosoma, which is not confined by the same limitations as our physical vision.

Then there was the visit to the Prambanan temples where I consciously tuned into the Shiva statue and was overwhelmed by its distinct and somewhat awe-inspiring energetic emanations. Or the time a few of us were meditating at a small temple at Borobodur, and other tourists, upon entering, whispered, 'Shhh … they are meditating.' The words felt as if they penetrated my core, leaving me feeling vulnerable and exposed to external energies. And then there were the discussions we had with Pak Suyono about non-physical life, karma, and so on. All in all, probably nothing earth-shattering for anybody with a background in esoteric ideas, but for me at that time it was revolutionary. It opened the door to previously unconscious drivers from my own past and to an energetic reality that was both awesome and that required careful management and self-protection. Shanti Loka literally provided a kick-start and the first unraveling of karmic ties I hadn't previously known that I had.

I also started to appreciate the fact that there might be such things as extraphysical consciousnesses and that they could interact with the physical world. There were various times when I was physically by myself in my room or in the meditation hall when I would feel quite certain that there was somebody present who was watching me. There was also the case of a German eccentric, an artist who occasionally visited Shanti Loka. He claimed to be able to paint two paintings at the same time, one with each hand, while possessed by extraphysical consciousnesses. I had the distinct impression that Pak Suyono disapproved of this practice and, without the matter being discussed, I understood that some engagements with extraphysical consciousnesses could be detrimental to our mental and emotional well-being. On the other hand, they could also be beneficial. Pak Suyono told the story of how the Findhorn community in Scotland was started when the founder had an encounter with an extraphysical consciousness who was rather like the Greek god Pan. So I began thinking about the relationship between our intraphysical consciousnesses and the extraphysical consciousnesses that seemed to be all around us.

I left two weeks earlier than I had planned. My reasoning was that I needed to return to my girlfriend if I wanted to save our relationship. I had dreamt of her with another man, and this dream had left me feeling uneasy and restless. As it was, I had already changed more than our relationship could support, and we soon separated. On one level, I was deeply upset by this break-up, but a part of me knew that if I wanted to pursue the new inner life that was opening up for me, there was no other option. Being single meant I could devote my time to meditation and study of relevant literature, trying to understand my new perceptions of the extraphysical dimension. It also meant I could go through periods of seeming neurosis and profound personality shifts without having to navigate another person's expectations of who I was.

Chapter 4

Searching and Unraveling

On my return to England, I spent two to three hours meditating every day. In hindsight, I don't know whether that much time was really needed for the processes that were unfolding, but I felt I needed it to cope. Every time I left the house I was overwhelmed by the simple experience of being among people. I seemed to perceive more things than I used to, but I was often confused about whether certain things were in fact genuine perceptions or merely my imagination. For example, when talking with people, I would sometimes observe brief but noticeable changes in their faces, often in response to particular moods or occurring at the same time as the person was making a statement reflecting a certain mental posture. At one level, this simply reflected the fact that I was becoming more present to people and noticing things I had previously missed. But sometimes, while a person was talking there also seemed to be distinct energetic changes, and I started to wonder whether perhaps there were extraphysical consciousnesses who were somehow interacting with and influencing the person at those times. At other times, I would leave an interaction feeling altered, as if I had taken something on from the person.

One of the more dramatic instances of this occurred when I went to see a lecturer about an assignment right after spending time in meditation. I was feeling very expansive and at peace when I entered his office. On the surface, our conversation was simply about the project, but shortly after we started talking, I noticed a sudden change in his facial expression and then something literally seemed to be flying from him towards me and attaching itself to me. It felt as if this 'something' was angry and irritated by me, and I was taken aback. Was I imagining things? The sense of irritation was certainly persistent, and I needed to find a quiet spot to meditate in order to help restore my balance. I now understand that a disturbed extraphysical consciousness who had been linked to my lecturer had attached itself to me, but at the time I did not know what was going on. While there were not many instances where I perceived the multidimensional interaction as clearly as on that occasion, the general dynamic of having my emotions strongly impacted when I spent time with other people happened almost every day. After years of feeling comfortably at home in pubs, I now struggled with the experience of spending time in them socially before feeling the urge to flee home to my own space and my meditation practice.

On the one hand, I was overwhelmed by the lack of mental and emotional boundaries I seemed to have in relation to the world. On the other, the realization that 'my' thoughts might not necessarily be my own but might be coming from the outside was also somewhat liberating. I realized that when I was writing essays, for example, some ideas just seemed to come out of nowhere. I would surprise myself with what I had written, and I had to think of the painter in Indonesia who channeled his artwork. Could I be 'channeling' some of these ideas? Similarly, I could be in a conversation, and things would come out of my mouth that made me somewhat uncomfortable because they might perhaps have hurt the other person's feelings. What if I was being influenced by an extraphysical consciousness even in the things I said? This is where it became confusing because I was not clear enough about my own independent patterns of thought and emotion to feel sure about which feelings, thoughts and words were coming from me and which might be coming from outside of me. One thing was certain. I lacked a healthy energetic boundary, not only in relation to other physical people but also to extraphysical beings. Meditation seemed like a refuge and a way of clearing out all the energies I felt I had picked up in the outside world. I also considered it important to continue the deeper inner cleansing process that had started at Shanti Loka. While I still experienced regular pressure around the area of my frontochakra, most of the energetic activity during that period seemed to be around my lower chakras, that is, the root and abdominal chakras. I would perceive such activity as drill-like pressure, vibrations and rotating currents, often accompanied by intense heat. The dominant emotions that arose during this period were anger and fear. It seemed as if, little by little, I was experiencing a kind of energetic therapy during my meditation that was an essential first step before the energetic focus could move to what is often referred to as the 'higher chakras' of the heart, throat, third eye and crown.

Earlier Experiences

In hindsight, I realize that this period of confusion and overwhelm was an important transition period. Up until then, my priorities in life had revolved, to put it bluntly, around sex, drugs and rock and roll. I knew that path had run its course, and for the last two years before heading to Shanti Loka, I had experienced major existential malaise. My final years of high school saw me more focused on drugs and alcohol than on school. After I miraculously graduated, I spent three years traveling, doing odd jobs, and continuing with the drinking and the drugs. It started off as fun, but over time I became seriously depressed. At 22 I felt old, as if I had done all there was to do in life, with no vision for a meaningful future. I simply could not see the point to life.

Then I started hearing voices. One day, while I was living in the Netherlands, I was walking along a canal when I felt a heavy presence behind me and clearly and menacingly heard my name being called. I turned around to see nothing. Shaken, I fled home to hide, suddenly no longer able to cope with being in public spaces. During this same period, I would lie in bed at night for hours trying to get to sleep but unable to because of the cacophony of voices running through my head, speaking incomprehensible words in another language and simply not shutting up. Yet, I continued with the alcohol and the drugs! They brought temporary relief by helping me sleep, but they did nothing to more permanently improve the state of my mind.

Somehow in the midst of this, there were moments when I felt that I was receiving intangible help. Like the time when I felt I was going completely crazy because the voices in my head would not stop their negative mental barrage of, 'You're crazy', 'You have no friends', 'You can't do anything', 'You're lost', 'You're crazy', and on and on (a serious case of consciential intrusion, something I'll explain in Chapter 14). I thought my head would explode when suddenly, for no apparent reason, a soothing calm descended upon my room and my mind (consciential assistance), and I could relax for the first time in days. On another occasion, I was caught in one of my frequent 'nightmares' (what I now understand as projections to very pathological dimensions). I found myself on a rocky plain scattered with large boulders that somehow felt extremely sinister. Suddenly the boulders began to morph into giant creatures, menacing and intent on smashing me. Lava was running over the rocks, and I was about to be grabbed and dragged down into the same sphere that these beings came from. As panic gripped my mind, a figure appeared, dancing and surrounded by a circle of flames. He dispelled the creatures and brought great calm to my mind. I awoke feeling both shaken by the initial part of the dream and protected, as though I had been saved by someone. It was not until much later, when I was staying at Shanti Loka, that I realized the resemblance between the figure who had helped me in my dream and the common depiction of Shiva dancing amid a ring of fire.

There were also times during this period when I would have a deep inner knowing that there was something I was meant to be doing and that somehow I needed to get my life on track so that

I could do whatever it was. The first step to achieving stability in my life was to engage in some kind of meaningful activity, so eventually I enrolled in Social Anthropology at the University of Kent at Canterbury. I thought that seeing through a formal education would provide me with an anchor, which it did, and happily it has led to my current profession. But the real transformation was not caused by academia. I started life at university much as I had been leading it up until then, drinking and smoking excessively. But the pressure became unbearable. I would sit in a room with another eight or nine guys, smoking dope and feeling paralyzed and paranoid. Or I would go out, get drunk and worry about my sudden aggressive outbursts.

At long last, the penny dropped. I needed to stop doing this to myself. I think the fact that I had a new relationship with a girl who neither drank nor smoked drugs played an important role. It opened me up to the amazing revelation that there was actually another way, that what for so many years had been my way of life was really just one way of life and not *the* way of life. And almost as soon as I stopped completely muddling my own mind, new people came into my life who led me to Shanti Loka.

* * *

I have provided this bit of background because I think it helps in understanding my state of mind when I returned from Shanti Loka. A new vista of life was opening before me, but I still had strong patterns from this immediate lifetime to deal with, not to mention other baggage I may have been carrying from previous ones. Cannabis had absolutely no attraction for me anymore, as I feared the effect it had had on my mind. But I did indulge in a few more drunken nights. One evening when I was lying down to sleep after drinking with some other students, I applied the technique I had learned at Shanti Loka to remarkable effect. I became very aware of my body being drunk, but experienced myself as separate as I observed my body's drunken state. I did not realize this at the time, but I had separated ever so slightly with my psychosoma from my physical body, and my consciousness, which was projected in the psychosoma, was feeling the body 'from the outside'. This was one of the last times I ever got drunk. My new personality, or maybe it was my true personality, gradually took over as I continued to meditate and clear layer upon layer of blocked energies from my energetic system.

It was difficult and a bit lonely to be doing this kind of work by myself, however, and I started looking for others who shared this interest and could perhaps guide me and help me understand some of the more intense changes that were happening to me. For a small town, Canterbury has a remarkable collection of spiritual groups. I attended sessions on Native American spirituality, including a sweat lodge. I went to UFO talks, channeling sessions, and *A Course in Miracles* workshops.

For a while, I found more enduring companionship with a Mahayana Buddhist group. I felt a little self-conscious on my first visit to a proper religious group, but that did not last long. I appreciated the humor and the psychological perspective of the weekly talks, which took me beyond the narrow confines of my physical identity to something larger, the idea of the Buddha mind. I also appreciated the focus on compassion and the emphasis that the purpose of the spiritual path must be for the benefit of others. Those things resonated very well with me and I liked the context and intention they gave to my meditation practice. What resonated less well was the encouragement to submit my spiritual journey to the particular lama at the head of this lineage. I did not want him as my guru.

Then I visited another group and learned about Zen Buddhism. Soon after that, I started my day with an hour of *zazen*, the Zen sitting meditation that focuses on the breath. I would follow this by a walk, which in turn would be followed by the Shanti Loka B-ing meditation. Zen Buddhism shared with Shanti Loka an emphasis on being aware of the body and the world, and this simple practice seemed to expand my consciousness and give me access to new insights. I still recall the feeling of clarity when I watched ripples forming in a pool of water after I had thrown a rock into it. It made me realize that we move through life causing ripples in the energetic fabric of time and space that have repercussions on levels we do not even imagine. Or the time when I was watching a sunset at the beach and suddenly realized that the rays of the sun that were shining directly at me were actually doing the same for everybody, and that in fact each and every one of us is the center of the universe with infinite unconditional love shining on us, whether we realized it or not. These insights felt very profound, as did others I gained from studying certain Buddhists texts.

But there were significant aspects of my own experiences that Buddhism, or at least the teachings I had access to, did not help me understand better. These included the types of energetic influences I described earlier, but they also included the projective experiences I was having during this period. On the advice of Pak Suyono, I had developed a practice of being aware of my body while falling asleep. What this did, unbeknown to me at the time, was to help me take my awareness into the sleep state and the psychosoma. While falling asleep, my chakras would become active, especially the frontochakra. Sometimes this would be followed by the sense of a bright light. This usually caused me to open my physical eyes to see if there was any light, but there never was. At times, I would have the awareness of my physical body being asleep while my mind was wide awake, and I would experience intense dreams of flying or meeting people who seemed very real. On one occasion, I had gone to sleep repeating a Buddhist mantra ('*Om mani padme hum*') over and over in my mind. I became conscious very briefly of being in a large hall filled with Buddha statues before returning to physical

39

awareness, where I awoke with a huge smile on my face and tingling all over my body, as if I had just been bathed in beautiful and intense energies.

But it seemed that for the Buddhist teachers these things were irrelevant. They were all just phenomena and illusion like the physical world, and they were equally likely to pose a distraction on the path to enlightenment and the awareness of our true nature as a manifestation of the Buddha mind. I could follow that theory, but it did not really satisfy me. I wanted to understand what was going on.

Despite this, I continued to feel very at home and blissful during the Buddhist meditation sessions, and I even considered life in a Buddhist monastery after university. But then I met Leia, who had a profoundly transformative effect on me. It was through spending time with her that my energies moved upwards, leading to an 'opening of the head' through unprecedented expansions of consciousness.

PART 3

NEW HORIZONS AND LOTS OF ENERGY!

Chapter 5

My First Encounter with a Walk-In

This part of the book deserves its own reminder: Don't believe anything I say! It's definitely a bit 'out there'. Some of what follows is what I saw and experienced, but other things are based on what I was told, and even I am not sure I believe all of that. For example, Leia's claim to being a 'new consciousness' is quite implausible from the evolutionary perspective of conscientiology, and whether walk-ins really exist is also contentious. I do know though, that she had very powerful energy and was extremely psychic. I saw plenty of evidence to satisfy me of that. I did, however, sometimes have the feeling that her 'teachings' were designed more to challenge conventional wisdom and force people to reconsider things than to always be factually accurate.

By her own account, Leia was a walk-in. When she first opened her eyes, she saw a whirl of energy with no distinguishable features. As she put it later, 'It makes it hard to put your lipstick on when you don't know where your lips are.' She soon learned to make out the material world, but from what I could gather, the world as seen by most of us is only a very small part of what is seen by Leia.

Leia was 'born' or, perhaps more appropriately, 'walked into' her body' on June 30, 1992. When I first met her in 1996, she was four years old. You wouldn't have guessed it though, because the body in which she was manifesting was 38 at the time. Prior to Leia's arrival, this body had been occupied by Linda. My information about Linda is scant. Leia described Linda as a regular young girl, slightly rebellious perhaps, but very practical and not in any way interested in spiritual matters. Sometime during her twenties, however, strange events started to take over her life. Linda began hearing voices, and one day she awoke with the entire text of the Bible etched in her mind. She developed clair-voyant abilities, seemingly spontaneously, and applied these within the framework that offered itself most naturally in her circumstances, the English Spiritualist Church. Like other spiritualist groups, the English Spiritualist Church uses the Bible as its guiding text but focuses especially on those passages that describe Jesus and others having psychic experiences. Its services incorporate psychic healing and communication with extraphysical consciousnesses. Linda became a regular medium during church services. Eventually, her psychic powers must have become remarkable. According to Leia, Linda caused a storm during one particularly dry summer, and she could change traffic lights with her mind to suit her needs when in a hurry. Linda also had a husband and a son.

Gradually, Linda became aware of the program that she had set for her life. Her body was to become the vehicle for another consciousness, Leia, who would 'walk' into it. What this meant, for Linda, was that she herself first had to vacate the premises, so to speak. As the story was told, Linda and her husband brought a friendly doctor on board. The dramatic changes that occurred with Linda over a relatively short period of time meant that her husband had become used to many seemingly strange events. I expect that she would have had a similar effect on other people touched by her presence, and I can only assume that the doctor was such a person. The doctor's role was to keep the body alive for the short period of time, approximately three minutes, between Linda's conscious exit from it in her psychosoma and Leia's newly entering psychosoma as it reoccupied and thus re-energized it. For this to occur, Linda must have had the ability to consciously leave her body for good. That is, through the power of her own will, she 'died' voluntarily by rupturing the silver cord of energies that connects the psychosoma to the soma. Then Leia, also through the power of her will, 'entered' the body.

The exchange of bodily occupants apparently took place

without a hitch, but when Linda's son first met Leia he noticed immediately that this was not his mummy. Not surprisingly, he was quite distressed. He recovered quickly, however, and adjusted to the fact that he now had two mothers, one here and another on 'the other side'. It no doubt helped that he too was particularly psychic. When I first met him, he was about nine or ten, and his playmates were for the most part extraphysical consciousnesses. He received home education, and his teacher once mentioned to me that it was very important to keep the answers out of your mind when you were teaching him, because otherwise he would just mentally pluck them from you.

Because the body now occupied by Leia had been formed by another consciousness, it was regularly trying to expel her. I understand that there was one incident some time prior to my meeting her when she was seriously ill and the body almost succeeded. As she put it, 'For you, it is hard to leave the body; for me it is hard to stay inside the body.'

I know this all sounds rather strange, because I still remember how I reacted when I first heard about Leia. The person who first told me about her was a university friend. She was a lovely girl and had been the first person to introduce me to spiritual concepts in general, even before I visited Shanti Loka. But she was also 'away with the fairies'. She was perhaps the least grounded person I have ever met, and unfortunately, when you get involved in multidimensional matters, lack of groundedness can have very negative consequences. Imagine, for example, if my reaction to those plastic bags in Indonesia had become a chronic condition. I now believe that our mental institutions are full of people who have perceptions of more subtle dimensions but no suitable way of integrating them with their physical reality, and perhaps more often than not, it is the 'dark side' of other dimensions that these people perceive. So when this friend first told me about Leia, I was convinced that she had lost it. By her account, Leia was an apparently superhuman being that knew the past and the future of each and every individual as well as the answer to any question one might have. Well, perhaps she did not exactly know it herself, but she had access to the information at will because she had a direct connection to the 'Akashic records', a hypothetical extraphysical repository of all information about every consciousness. I was very skeptical and in no particular hurry to meet this person. I myself had recently settled into the local Buddhist group and was feeling quite comfortable there. I meditated a lot, practiced mindfulness and was anxious not to be concerned with outlandish New Age ideas. I certainly did not feel that I needed the assistance of some strange psychic person who surely could not be for real.

A few weeks later, however, Leia was giving a public talk in a community center in Canterbury. I remember being both excited and reluctant all the way to the venue, wondering why I was bothering to go, yet feeling that this was deeply important. The talk was attended by about 50 people, a large crowd for this kind of thing in Canterbury. It was opened by two young women who told us about how they had been taken up into spaceships for experiments that involved the removal of an ovary for one of them. This was explained as stemming from the desire of that particular extraterrestrial race to crossbreed with humans. I had never heard of these ideas, and they certainly challenged my paradigm at the time. This challenge took new heights during the talk given by Leia, undoubtedly the energetic epicenter of the evening. Following the girls' account of their abductions, she introduced herself as an alien. I am not quite sure why. Perhaps it was to distinguish herself from normally born humans or merely because her talk was hosted by a UFO group, or perhaps she was alluding to the extraterrestrial origin of her consciousness. From that perspective, we are all extraterrestrials.

The specific details of that talk are not clear to me anymore. I heard Leia speak many times afterwards, and she often said very similar things. One thing I remember well is the exceptionally buoyant mood of the audience. Looking around during and after Leia's talk, I noticed that the audience gave the impression of being extremely relaxed yet exhilarated and even mildly euphoric. People mingled freely during the break, and I certainly did not feel any of the inhibitions I often felt and observed in others at public gatherings when one finds oneself talking with strangers. I did feel such inhibitions, however, about approaching Leia. I was keen to speak to her but also felt incredibly shy. I was talking with a couple of people when I looked across at her and saw her glancing at me, though only for an instant. In that moment there was a sudden burst of energy from my solar plexus. It felt as if I had been opened up, with energy flowing freely where it hadn't before. I felt extremely euphoric for the remainder of the evening and for some days afterwards as a result of this energetic release. I attribute this experience to some energetic action taken by Leia when she looked at me.

Through friends, I learned that it was possible to organize personal consultations with Leia, and eventually, after much internal resistance, I did so. I was planning to go to Mexico for the next summer break and wanted her guidance about this trip. When I think about it now, organizing a trip to Mexico seems like a rather straightforward thing to do, but at that point in my life, I was in many ways still very neurotic. I felt as if I was being driven to go, and I could not work out by what or why I should do it at all. So this was one question I carried to Leia. I was incredibly nervous at this first private meeting. It was uncanny to be in the presence of somebody who you realized very quickly could read your every thought, especially when your thoughts seemed to constantly gravitate towards sexual fantasies about that person. But what could I do? I had to just accept myself, trust that Leia would not mind, and keep working at focusing my thoughts on the actual topics I wanted to discuss.

In many ways, I found the realization that there are people

who can look into our innermost minds very liberating. While it encouraged me to be more diligent about the contents of my mind, it also helped me to accept what I found there. Knowing that I was unavoidably sharing my mind with others meant that there was no point in being coy or self-deceiving. I don't think that I have been in the presence of a living mind-reader of that caliber for many years now (although, of course, you can never be certain), but I now know that there are extraphysical people around me at all times to whom physical humans are open books. I also know that, even if the people around me do not consciously know what I am thinking, many do in fact pick up unconsciously on the thoughts of those around them. Our inter-personal dynamics are greatly determined by unspoken aspects of our interactions.

One of the things I still recall from this first conversation with Leia was her account about how she needed to adjust to the physical dimension. Not only did she need to adjust her visual perception to allow her to properly focus on material objects among all the other energies she perceived, but she also needed to adjust herself to dealing with human beings. She said that at first she would give people what she thought were clear sugges-tions on how to alter their lives for the better, only to have them respond that they could not make the recommended adjustments for one reason or another. Leia had to learn about the power of emotional factors in human life and that, while it might be the best thing for you to quit your job or leave your partner or move to another city, factors of attachment, fear of the unknown, and other emotional reactions have a very real sway over human beings. From a purely 'rational' perspective of a detached consciousness, certain actions might seem logical, but for them to work in the actual life circumstances of a human being, the matter might sometimes need to be tackled from another angle.

There may have been other points as well, but they have become blurred with information provided on other occasions.

On the whole, this first encounter was very narrowly focused on my journey to Mesoamerica. She told me that Mexico had followed the pattern of other ancient cultures. According to Leia, the temple cities that we marvel at today were built by a particular group of consciousnesses of extremely advanced spiritual evolution. In this culture, people were divided into three principal groups: the priests, or religious specialists; the traders; and the farmers. This initial civilization existed for only a relatively short period, a few hundred years maybe. They had a limited mandate, as it were. Other people (or rather, other consciousnesses) with a more restricted vision of power took control. It was this new set of consciousnesses who started using human sacrifices, a practice that still dominated much of Mexico when the Spanish arrived. Leia also told me that I was driven to visit this part of the world because of some past lives I apparently experienced there that had made a strong impact on my consciousness, in part through some (unspecified) negative actions on my part. I later learned through my own experiences that the cleansing that had started at Shanti Loka related to at least one of those lives.

Chapter 6

Journey to Mesoamerica

The reason I was going to Mexico, or so I tried to convince myself rationally, was to learn about the Zapatista uprising that was happening in Chiapas in the southern part of the country. I was quite taken by the enigmatic and eloquent figure of Subcomandante Marcos, a character who always appeared in a balaclava, made rousing and insightful statements about the impact of the global capitalist economic system on indigenous communities in Mexico, and in January 1994, led Mayan communities in a peaceful yet revolutionary occupation of San Cristóbal de las Casas, the capital of Chiapas. My plan had been to volunteer with an organization that provided aid to the indigenous communities affected by the subsequent government crackdown.

On another level, even before visiting Leia, I felt like I was taking a journey into my own past. There is an interesting relationship between space-time and multidimensionality. As we go through our many lifetimes in human form, we naturally experience different cultures and geographic regions. Do we need to return physically to all of these regions if we want to address the karma we created there? For consciousnesses who are fully aware of their multidimensional being, journeys through physical space may be quite unnecessary, unless they need to take specific physical actions, such as reconnecting in person with old evolutionary colleagues or establishing particular physical institutions or structures in a specific location for karmic reasons. I am not yet at that level of consciousness, but I am nonetheless uncertain that I needed to physically go to Mesoamerica to address my karmic debt or trigger significant memories. I think I could probably have done it elsewhere simply by dealing with the internal energetic, mental and emotional patterns that were linked to my past in that physical space. And yet I believe that being physically present in that space made experiences and connections available to me that I would not otherwise have had and thereby accelerated the process of transforming those energetic patterns. One of the exciting aspects of being in the intraphysical dimension in our current era is our global mobility and the possibilities this opens up for us to connect both with unprecedented numbers of other consciousnesses and with significant locations from our own multiexistential past. In other words, we now have the opportunity to resolve karmic issues with more people and in more places than ever before.

I had a lot of fear surrounding this journey. It was in many ways irrational, but it was visceral and dominated my body even though my mind reasoned against it. Of course, some external factors contributed as well. Before I left Europe, my mother, in a gesture of motherly concern, sent me an article about the crime and violence in Mexico City. When I got to Mexico City, people warned me against going to Chiapas because it was so dangerous. And when I got to Chiapas, I received the same warning about traveling further south to Guatemala. Each person I spoke with seemed to consider the next unknown to be dangerous.

For me, this trip was a significant exercise in growing my trust in multidimensional assistance. I traveled without a Lonely Planet guide and without any research, simply going with the flow. I would not travel like this again, as I prefer some level of planning these days, but it worked fine, and it gave me a sense of being connected with multidimensional guidance, which seemed to manifest in a range of ways. A couple of other European tourists I met in Oaxaca told me about a meditation center in Guatemala, where I ended up spending the better part of a month. When I spent a week with a family in San Cristóbal de las

Casas, the mother of the house was just leaving for England to go on a retreat with the same Buddhist lama with whom I had just been in retreat some months previously. And so it went, meeting significant people and going to great places simply by following what seemed right at the moment.

My first striking multidimensional experience on this journey occurred on my first visit to one of the temple sites. As I crossed the large plaza of the temple overlooking Oaxaca, an extra-physical man approached me, coupled himself with my energies and walked with me for a while. I did not physically see him, but I could feel him within my body, yet he was clearly separate. He was short, not even up to my shoulders, and my impression was that he had been around those pyramids for a long time, that he was an original inhabitant. It was incredibly tangible but also fairly uneventful. I did not receive any significant information or insight into the temple's history from him. It was almost as if he had just come along to say hello, and after a few minutes he left again.

By the time I arrived in San Cristóbal, I had already decided that I would not be volunteering with an aid organization. I believed that their work was important, but it simply did not seem like it was the right work for me. Instead, I wanted to go to the meditation center in Guatemala. I still went through the motions, though, and spoke with some people who placed volunteers in Mayan communities, but it turned out my Spanish was not good enough in any event.

Somewhere along the way, I had an experience that made my hair stand on end. I was in a bus next to a couple of Mayan women who were whispering to each other in their own language. Although I could not understand them they sounded incredibly familiar to me, and I realized that it was this sound, this whispering in that language, that I had heard in my head on those dreadful sleepless nights in the Netherlands when I thought I was going crazy from the voices that wouldn't stop. It was at that moment that I fully realized the significance of my karmic debt here. While this is conjecture to some extent, the pieces fit nicely: the comments by Pak Suyono about dabbling in occult forces for a negative purpose as well as those by Leia about having engaged in some negative actions here; the voices in my head; the pull to come to this part of the world; and the history of human sacrifices in Mayan temples! I had in some past life committed these acts of violence in pursuit of spiritual power. By doing so, I had bound myself to the consciousnesses I had harmed. The voices I had heard in my head had been from other dimensions. They had been the voices of people I had sacrificially murdered and who now were, consciously or unconsciously, attached to me. I wanted to make amends in this lifetime.

The best way to do so, it seemed to me, was to try to balance the energies I had created in this environment hundreds of years ago by generating positive energies in the same geographic area this time round. So I spent a lot of time focusing on positive energy during this trip. 'All you need is love' was my mantra as I walked around the streets of San Cristóbal while focusing on sending out this energy. I would spend an hour or more every day practicing the B-ing meditation wherever I was staying and, in the Buddhist tradition, I focused on making my energy available to all beings. When I eventually arrived at the Las Pyramides Meditation Center on the shore of Lake Atitlán in Guatemala, I participated in chanting and meditation sessions, and whenever I visited the old temple sites, I deliberately tried to exteriorize, or send out, energy that would counteract the negative energy of cruelty that had been generated at so many of them.

I visited a number of ancient Mayan temple sites: Tikal, Palenque, Yaxchilán, Bonampak, and one or two others. My experiences were varied. I rarely felt at peace at the temples themselves; rather, I felt like I needed to give constant attention to my own energies and those around me. On the other hand, I felt good in the areas surrounding the temples, such as the campsites where I stayed, and I experienced numerous profound expansions of consciousness there. These experiences led me to accept Leia's depiction of two waves of consciousnesses having occupied these areas. The more recent wave, who used human sacrifice, left significant energetic baggage, but underlying this were the more refined energies produced by the previous consciousnesses. From the physical perspective, we would call all these people 'Maya', but from the multidimensional perspective, we may well be dealing with consciousnesses of quite different evolutionary levels.

I spent four weeks at the Las Pyramides Meditation Center. The center was run by a Guatemalan woman, with the support of a young Englishman. He ran the yoga sessions every morning, and she led evening classes on a range of topics, from past lives and karma to chakras. The first week of my stay was spent fasting and in silence, not a requirement but a recommended way of acclimatizing. I recall the feelings of hunger, which people said would go away but did not for me. They led me to 'dream' incessantly about food. Some years later, I learned that I was not actually dreaming but that my psychosoma had left my body and, on the urging of my desires, was eating imaginary food. If we become conscious of this, we can actually use this physical desire as a projective technique, but at that point I was unaware of this. Las Pyramides, in the heartland of my Mayan past, was a perfect place for me to stay. I did not get the same energetic charge from the people running the place that I had felt from Leia or Pak Suyono, but it was nonetheless a memorable period that led to some retrocognitions and other experiences. I was not looking for another teacher at that stage, anyway, because I felt as if I had Leia's presence in my mind.

In fact, throughout the whole journey, it seemed like I was telepathically connected to Leia. When I encountered areas at some of the temple sites that made my hair stand on end, I would connect with her energies while exteriorizing positive energy in an attempt to cleanse the space. When I was unsure which way to go or whom to speak to, I would often perceive her voice like a reassuring presence in the back of my mind. Is it possible that I was imagining this? Yes, it is, but for me it was distinctly present from the time I first visited Leia until shortly after my move to Brazil about a year later. For this whole period, Leia seemed to be 'in my head'. Her presence quite often expressed itself through jokes at my expense that seemed to arise in my mind, but reflected her distinct humor and took my perspective of myself far beyond the small concerns that seemed so real and important to me at the time, thereby helping me to see myself more as a multidimensional consciousness than a small intraphysical personality. When this presence eventually faded, its absence was just as noticeable as its presence.

Some years before personally embarking on an exploration of consciousness, I happened to read the works of Carlos Castaneda, an anthropologist who had supposedly apprenticed himself to a Mexican shaman. Now an anthropology student myself and with an interest in the multidimensional, it is perhaps not surprising that the thought of a similar apprenticeship in Mexico had crossed my mind. The father of the host family I stayed with in San Cristóbal de las Casas was a medical practitioner who was involved in cross-cultural work with local Mayan *curanderos* (healers). He warned me that some of these shamans were not necessarily 'nice' people. He told me of an incident when he had felt himself being energetically drained during a meeting with a group of curanderos. Eventually, he was able to identify the man who was consciously depleting his energies, and he thought it was in response to an unintended slight. Despite this warning, I visited two Mayan shamans, but always with my energetic guard up.

I was taken to the first as part of a guided tour of the traditional Mayan town of San Juan Chamula. He was a middle-aged man whom we visited while he was conducting a healing ritual to help a man retrieve a part of his spirit. Such spirit loss is considered a classic cause of disease among Mayan curanderos. On the same tour, we also visited the famous Chamula church with its mix of Catholic effigies and Mayan rituals, including the sacrifice of live chickens and possibly other animals. The energy in the church was quite distinct. There was a definite power to it, but it also felt dirty or false, like a power maliciously obtained. The sacrifice of live animals was too reminiscent of the ancient custom of human sacrifice and did not sit well with me.

Despite these reservations, I still returned to Chamula to meet the shaman and ask him whether I could learn from him. The situation was similar to the one with the aid agency. On some deeper level, I had already decided that I was not really going to study with him, yet I felt the need to go through the motions of this previously held intention. The shaman, for his part, seemed quite open to the idea. I almost had the impression he had been waiting for me. He was standing outside his house when I arrived and seemed not in the least surprised to see me again. He suggested that I would need to learn his native language if I wanted to study with him. I do not recall exactly how I ended our interaction, but I do know that it was quite abrupt. I also left without paying him for his time, even though I knew that it was expected of people to pay a shaman even for something that was more like a social visit than a consultation. As I left, I could tell that I had offended him.

That night was incredibly intense. I know I was projected, but I had only a very vague recall of the event. When I awoke, I had a strong sense of having been under extraphysical attack all night. I also felt as if I had benefited from strong extraphysical protection. As usual on this journey, I had felt very close to Leia, whose presence I perceived as an energetic shield. When I checked my wallet later that day, I was sure that a sum of money was missing. Of course, I may have been mistaken about how much money I originally had, but I was pretty sure that an equivalent of about $20 had gone missing. Could the shaman have come to take his pay, and would he have caused me energetic harm had I not been so well supported? Possibly. It was certainly not the only time over the years that I had the sense of objects dematerializing.

My next encounter with a shaman was friendlier. In a small town in Guatemala, a local 'amateur' tourist guide took me and another tourist to a local curandero, a wizened old man who held a small ceremony to ensure us a safe journey and a successful life. He chanted, burned copal incense (traditional incense derived from a tree resin), poured libations and, at the end, rubbed his hand quite vigorously over our foreheads in the area associated with the frontochakra. It was as if he wanted to energize that area. I do not recall perceiving any particular sensations during the ceremony, but that night I awoke with the smiling face of the old curandero still before my eyes and the tingling of energy running through my body, and I knew he had visited me outside of the body. And even though I again could not recall the actual projection, the energetic sensation showed me clearly that it had been a positive encounter.

There was one other thing I wanted to experience in Mexico, and this too had been influenced by reading Carlos Castaneda. I was drawn to the peyote desert in the northern part of the country. My entry point was the regional capital, San Luis Potosí. Again, I had not thought out a plan and simply arrived in the city. I soon met another foreigner with a similar intention, although his desire for peyote was more recreational. Soon we were on a train to Wadley, a small village in the desert. Two local recreational peyote seekers attached themselves to us, and before long, my three companions were sharing whiskey and talking about smoking a joint. This was not at all the energy I wanted to be around, and once we arrived in Wadley, I excused myself and found separate accommodation. For me, peyote, like all so-called 'hallucinogens', was a powerful substance that could connect me with multidimensionality, not something to be taken for a laugh or mixed with depressants such as alcohol and marijuana. I approached the plant with considerable respect and a sense that its misuse could cause psychological or even multidimensional harm.

The following day I equipped myself with two large bottles of water and some apples and headed into the desert. Not only did I find the peyote, but I also bumped into a large group of Huichol Indians engaged in their own peyote ritual. I knew they were not going to invite me, but I still felt privileged to be sharing the same space with a group of people who had used this substance as a pathway to multidimensional self-awareness for centuries. I ate some of my peyote buttons while watching the group from a distance and then moved on to find my own space for the night, which was essentially a night of projections. My only comforts were a sarong and my bag that served as a pillow as I lay under the stars, but my physical body was of little concern once the drug took effect.

I recall little detail other than the presence of a consciousness who felt ancient. At one point, I felt that I was this presence, and I laughed at the insignificance of my 'Kim' identity when contrasted with its ancientness. The following day I felt profoundly at peace with the world. I sat under a tree and looked across the desert, watching a donkey plod along. Everything seemed peaceful and softened. Eventually, I made my way back to the village. On my walk, I felt the presence of a distinct extra-physical consciousness: it was as if he *was* peyote.

The relationship between drugs like peyote and states of consciousness is fascinating. Usually termed 'hallucinogens', from a multidimensional perspective they are more accurately described as *projectiogens*, substances that cause us to project out of the physical body in our psychosoma, or sometimes even our mentalsoma. Yes, the drugs have a measurable impact on our nervous system, but they also have an impact on our subtle bodies, including our energetic system. Through absorbing the substance of the plant, we alter our vibratory frequency and connect with particular dimensions. Such experiences can be benign, but if our system is not prepared for them, they can also be highly traumatic. One of the reasons I would caution strongly against combining projectiogens with depressants such as alcohol and marijuana is that the latter two create links with denser dimensions and consciousnesses that may not have our best interests at heart. But even if we stick to the projectiogens themselves, their use should be treated with caution and respect.

Eventually, it seemed that my Mexican experience was complete, although I continued to regularly project to this area for months after my physical journey, reflecting my deep attachment. I left the country still feeling myself under the calming influence of the peyote dimension and returned to England and university. For some months, I did not think about visiting Leia. In fact, I felt as if there were no need for me to do so anymore. I was back to the comfortable place I had been before I first saw her. I was OK with my spiritual journey and did not need any external assistance. But gradually a niggle set in. I needed to grow more, and eventually I arranged to go to one of her weekly meetings.

Chapter 7

Leia's Life Task

It had been more than six months since I had last met Leia physically, although I felt myself in mental contact with her for most of that time. She assisted me in more than one projection of consciousness, and I had the impression of hearing her in my mind regularly. In February 1997, I started going to her place for informal weekly meetings which were frequented by up to a dozen or so people. These meetings were mainly social and provided an opportunity for meeting others with an interest in psychic matters as well as for receiving energization (similar to Reiki healing) from Leia. I also attended three or four meetings of her 'development group'. These took place monthly and involved psychic exercises and guided meditations, frequently with a focus on inducing retrocognitions (memories of past lives). My final meeting with Leia was in 1998, after I returned from my year of studying with Waldo Vieira in Brazil. In retrospect, my time with Leia was a period of profound personal shifts in consciousness, but before I describe my more significant personal experiences, I will summarize some of the key ideas that she introduced me to during this period.

Leia claimed that she had come to Earth with a very particular task. She often referred to herself as an 'experiment'. Although walk-ins have apparently existed at various places and times on Earth, there was something unique about her. Leia claimed to be a 'fresh consciousness', that is, she had never had any previous existences on this or any other planet. As she put it, she was taken straight from the Ultimate Being and put into the body in which I met her. Those conducting the experiment were a group of consciousnesses Leia called 'the Boardroom'. I am not clear on the specific details, but my impression is that this Boardroom is constituted of quite a number of consciousnesses. In my presence, however, Leia only ever referred to a few individuals who played a particular role in her existence. I can remember three: Isaac, Sophia and Astera.

Personally, I have no attachment to the Christian religion, so I never found this point particularly troublesome, but for others, what I am about to say might seem highly controversial. According to Leia, Isaac was the person who is commonly known as Jesus Christ. When I asked why she called him Isaac, she simply said, 'Because that is his name.' Leia suggested that the date usually ascribed to Jesus's life as being about 2000 years ago is completely off and that Isaac in fact lived approximately 3500 years ago. I have no idea about the accuracy of these assertions, and I have invested no energy in seeking to verify them. I recognize that the date is utterly at odds with the beliefs we hold, which I assume are based on some sort of record. On the other hand, I subsequently became aware of the theory that the story of Jesus is merely a rehashed version of a much older Egyptian story that also tells of a holy man who was killed and who rose again three days later. I have since wondered whether perhaps Leia's Isaac was the protagonist in this 'original' Jesus story. Whatever the status of Jesus/Isaac, I do know that there was an extra-physical consciousness who played a very important role in Leia's life. She would usually refer to him as her parent, often in the context of 'one does not choose them', as he had a rather mischievous sense of humor.

What she meant by calling him her parent was that he had been instrumental in orchestrating her intraphysical existence. He was also one of her son's extraphysical playmates and was generally around the place. He was regularly present at the meetings held at Leia's house and was said to have a liking for waistcoats and remote controls. The latter were popular targets for any mischief that he might play. On one occasion, a regular visitor at Leia's related how he had been unable to find the TV remote control for a week in his shared house, eventually finding it in a spot where he knew he had looked. This was attributed to Isaac, as was the disappearance for some time of the same person's waistcoat. This kind of disappearance and reappearance of material objects may sound fanciful, and maybe it was just a disorganized shared house, but over the years I have experienced too many curious disappearances of objects (sometimes, but not always, followed by their reappearance) to attribute all of them to mistaken perceptions. The phenomenon of dematerialization is well documented, and it seems to happen regularly around people who actively engage with extraphysical consciousnesses, especially humorous ones like Isaac.

Personally, I only had a couple of visual encounters with Isaac. Once, during my experimental phase with various mystical traditions, I went to sleep while repeating to myself, like a mantra, 'Jesus and I are one.' Shortly after falling asleep, I had a projection in which a giant caricature of a Jesus figure was dramatically waving his stigmata at me. I returned to my body somewhat disturbed but primarily embarrassed because I felt my ardent spiritual pursuit was being mocked. This was indeed the case, and while I felt embarrassed at the time, I can now see both the funny and the pragmatic side of this lesson. The next time I met Leia she apologized for Isaac's sense of humor without my having described the experience. Another time, my Zen meditation practice led to a sudden and intense rising of kundalini energy that left me ecstatic and feeling as if I was a living embodiment of the universe. This experience lasted for some hours. In the midst of it, I went to the beach and was sitting there just after sunset, grinning from ear to ear in a state of bliss, when I suddenly saw the figure of a man in a flowing robe walking on the water some 30 meters off the shore, waving at me merrily. Walking on water is the classic Jesus act, and again this appearance seemed to serve the dual purpose of reminding me not to take my spiritual experiences too seriously, while providing tangible evidence of a supportive extraphysical presence. I once asked Leia whether Isaac had had any intraphysical lives after his 'Jesus' appearance, and the answer was yes, either two or three (I am unsure now). Apparently, Isaac is not particularly impressed with the role attributed to his 'Jesus' existence by the wider society, and every year at Christmas time he flees the planet (extraphysically of course) to get away from the barrage of invocations. His real birthday, according to Leia, was January 26.

Another important member of the Boardroom was Sophia. This was the name by which Leia referred to planet Earth. Sophia had also been instrumental in initiating the experiment that was Leia. The experiment was required because Sophia had decided to accelerate her evolution, and this meant that the inhabitants of the planet would inevitably have to follow. As this was not occurring at what was considered the required speed, the Boardroom felt the need to support the human race in this process. To this end, they sought to create a pure channel through which to transmit information and energy to the global population. This channel, of course, was Leia. From my own perspective, other than the expansion of consciousness I would sometimes experience when contemplating a particularly beautiful natural environment or some of the energy centers I will describe shortly, I am not aware of ever having had any perceptions of Sophia as an individual consciousness.

Astera, another Boardroom member, also had a mischievous sense of humor. She was described as somebody whose last physical life on this planet had been in ancient Egypt as a half-human half-cat. This is a classic Egyptian character represented in art and statues, usually assumed to be a representation of an imaginary deity. According to Leia, such bodies did exist and were used as vehicles of manifestation by consciousnesses. Astera's particular trademark was intense sexual energy, something she would occasionally use to make people aware of her presence. She might also influence people's thoughts, something that could become noticeable when a conversation would suddenly drift in a humorously sexual direction. Unlike what might be called sexual intrusion, however, where a consciousness uses sexual energy to take something from another, Astera's energy was very positive, and her presence installed a sense of fun and lightness in people.

A more recent addition to the Boardroom was Linda. Apparently she was able to assume this position after the successful completion of her most recent life task, culminating in her conscious departure from her body so that Leia could use it. But why did this occur? As Leia put it, the Boardroom was concerned for the future of the planet. She suggested that this planet is very special and widely (i.e. intergalactically) known for its beauty. The destructive path that was now being followed by consciousnesses in human bodies had gotten so out of hand that it was increasingly out of sync with the energies of the planet, and substantial damage to the planet's body was indeed possible. The Boardroom was anxious to rapidly infuse a high dose of positive energy into the system. As the normal path through the birth canal is a comparatively slow process, they opted for the walk-in solution in order to fast-track the matter. In addition, the energy brought by Leia was unique, as she had not lived any physical lives prior to her appearance on this planet. Nor had she had any previous subtle or extraphysical existences as an individual entity. Rather, the Boardroom applied for and was granted (I never found out from whom) the right to create her by taking pure consciousness from what Leia called the 'Ultimate Being' and installing that into a human vehicle that was already physically and psychically developed. Her unique condition of being a totally new consciousness meant that she had no baggage or impurities, so there was a complete absence of personal karma. This had the benefit that Leia's energies were as pure as is possible in this dimension. Because of the absence of any personal karma, Leia was a clean slate. As she put it jokingly, 'I have never been a worm or a dog.' This would mean that she could come and do what she had to do and then go again, that is, deactivate her body for good. There was nothing holding her in this dimension. As it turned out, she did what she had to do but subsequently decided that she liked it here or at least wanted to hang around and be a mother to her son and a companion to Linda's husband. She suggested that she was engaging in certain activities, such as breeding horses, with the principal aim of creating karma for herself so as to strengthen her ties with the physical dimension.

The notion of a 'new' consciousness, manifesting such assistential energetic command as Leia, does not sit well with the model of the evolution of consciousness as described by conscientiology. According to this model, we are all moving from a level of extreme self-centeredness and rudimentary control over our energies of manifestation to ever increasing levels of awareness and assistance to others over the course of many thousands of lifetimes. But whatever one makes of her claim of being 'new', I was able to see the effect of her energies on many occasions. People regularly became slightly euphoric in her presence. Their psychic abilities were heightened and in my case, at least, negativity would all but vanish. After an evening at her place, sleep would often not come until early in the morning because my mind was buzzing and all my chakras pulsating almost to the point of discomfort. Yet the next day I'd bounce out of bed full of energy.

My understanding of her initial task is quite limited. I was told that there were other intraphysical people involved. Apparently, there had been a wealthy benefactor in the original plan. It was through him that contacts were made with world leaders, and Leia spent her first year traveling the planet talking to powerful and influential people. What exactly she told them I am not sure, but it would have concerned the future of the Earth and the need for countries to rethink their actions. Apparently, an attempt was made on her life at one point during the trip. Again, I do not know the details, but according to the story, Leia first thwarted the attack and then provided energetic healing to the failed assailants. After this trip, her allotted time was almost up. According to the original plan, she should have spent the remainder of her short life with the benefactor and then deactivated the body and returned to the source from which she came. But she refused. She often compared this part of her life with the kind of rebellion many humans go through as teenagers, when they go a different way from the one they might have had originally planned for themselves before birth. Leia spoke of heated arguments in the Boardroom. Some wanted to enforce the original scheme, while others suggested to just let her try it out. The latter prevailed, and so I and many others had the opportunity to meet her.

Chapter 8

Many Lives

One of the fundamental lessons conveyed by Leia was that life is multidimensional. Many of the ideas I got from talking with her were new to me, although I subsequently discovered that most had been around for a long time. While I had had many experiences of multidimensionality by the time I met Leia, I did not really have any idea of how to interpret them. In hindsight, I realized I had experienced many projections of consciousness, but at that point in time, I still did not really feel sure that I was not just dreaming. I had also started seeing auras and energies around people and things, and I could feel people's energies. But these experiences were not well integrated for me, and I regularly felt overwhelmed. Also, because nobody around me seemed to be having the same kinds of experiences, I oscillated between feeling as if there was something wrong with me and feeling rather special.

Leia's casual view on these phenomena helped me to both feel more normal and realize how little experience I really had in these matters. She spoke about all of us leaving the body every night, and for her, these out-of-body travels seemed to have a clarity that made them virtually indistinguishable from her daytime experiences. These were new ideas to me. Only later did I find many authors and meet other people who gave very similar accounts of their multidimensional experiences and shared the same vision of the 'afterlife' being really just that, a life after this one. It is different because it is lived without a physical body, but it is nonetheless not a state in which we are fundamentally transformed from who we are right here and now.

One could say that Leia was more from the extraphysical side than the physical one. She claimed never to have a loss of consciousness when she left her physical body and, in fact, found it easier to leave the body than to come back into it. Occasionally, she was not quite sure if she had seen somebody in the physical or the extraphysical state. One of the key points of her teachings, if one can really call her communications that, was that every human being has the same psychic potential as she does. All humans have the capacity to perceive extraphysical consciousnesses or gain insight into their own and others' past lives, and she assured us that we all leave our bodies, only with lesser degrees of awareness than her.

Leia did not provide any teachings about how to leave the body or maintain our awareness, but the development sessions she ran usually included a guided visualization that I subsequently understood as being aimed at inducing projections of consciousness. There are many benefits to consciously leaving the physical body. One of them is our ability to access memories from other lives. Think about it. This current physical body was not with us in previous lives. It has only been around since our last birth. Its memories are largely confined to those of our present life experiences (although our cells may carry much more ancient memories, but that is a different story again). The bodies I introduced earlier as the psychosoma and mentalsoma, however, have been with us throughout all our lifetimes. Under the right circumstances, we can access past-life memories when manifesting in those bodies. This seemed to be the primary purpose of applying the techniques during Leia's development sessions.

People sometimes have funny ideas about retrocognitions and past lives. I recall an English TV show at the time, where the skeptical host asked someone who believed in past lives why everybody who recalls them has always been a king or a queen and not just a peasant or a baker. Somehow this was considered to be an argument against the reality of the rebirth of consciousness. Another frequent argument against the idea of reincarnation is that population growth shows it to be false. This is really only an argument if you have an entirely materialistic perspective. Even at almost seven billion intraphysical people, the non-physical population significantly outnumbers the physical population on this planet. Once you realize this and you experience the vastness of extraphysical life, the argument makes no sense at all. As for the seeming claim to royalty by everybody who says that they recall their past lives, I have no doubt that there are people who claim to have been kings and queens when in fact they were no such thing. Others may have been royalty and feel themselves stuck trying to relive their former glory in this lifetime even when it is incongruous with their current life circumstances. In my retrocognitions, I felt and saw myself being all manner of people: an African peasant woman, a Japanese servant, a sailor, an Egyptian priest, a Buddhist monk as well as other people, both male and female, rich and poor, even from beyond this planet. There was little direct continuity in the external circumstances, but the inner circumstances, the thoughts and emotions those personalities experienced, seemed to represent a consistent pattern, aspects of which continued to manifest in my present life.

One of the benefits of having retrocognitions is that they can facilitate a cathartic release from unconsciously stored up energies that keep us stuck in emotional and mental patterns that we inherit from our own past lives. They can also help us understand our tendencies as well as our strengths and weaknesses, because the mental and emotional patterns we manifest today will be quite similar to those in our past. Retrocognitions can give us a real sense of perspective on the relevance of this current life and help us not to take life too seriously, while paradoxically increasing the value we give to the opportunities it offers. Awareness of our past lives will help us prioritize things that have lasting value, beyond the limits of this one physical existence. For example, gaining control over and positively transforming our mental and emotional patterns will be of benefit to us across lifetimes, unlike any material gain we might enjoy.

By her own account, Leia did not see people as most of us do but as the result of all the experiences the person has had throughout innumerable lifetimes. This means that she saw and understood the many intricate connections between lives in different times and circumstances. Occasionally, she would make reference to a past life that was currently dominating a person's manifestation. As she described it, most of us are dominated in our manifestations by a particular past life. For Leia, people appeared as pulsating energies with the dominant past life as the most prominent and immediately noticeable. Leia did not actually see faces as most of us do. Rather, she saw moving shapes of energy changing in accordance with the energetic stream affecting the person at any given moment. At least, that is how I imagined it based on her accounts.

I started to awaken to the very real impact that past lives have on us during my time at Shanti Loka. But it was through my exposure to the high-energy environment created by Leia that I really developed awareness of my own millennia-old history and past-life baggage. When Leia looked at me at that talk where I saw her for the first time, she affected something in me. I later understood that this was a continuation of the process that had started at Shanti Loka and concerned the cleansing or transformation of energies from a particular past existence.

There will be very few, if any, consciousnesses on this planet today who have not killed in the past. You might think of yourself as moral and good. You may consider yourself a pacifist and even be a vegetarian out of respect for the life of other beings. But we have all been here many, many times and have been both the victims and perpetrators of violence. It is part of the multidimensional human experience. My past actions seem to have got people seriously offside, to the extent that they persecuted me across lifetimes.

In this lifetime, the persecution was present right from the start. When I was a child, I 'dreamed' a lot. I frequently had flying dreams. I also repeatedly had a dream where I visited an underwater world. I always enjoyed these visits, because the world was very beautiful and it felt as if I was returning home. I did not always enjoy the flying dreams as they often involved fleeing from people who wanted to hurt me. I recall at around the age of six waking up from a 'dream' screaming because a large group of people had gathered around me and were stabbing me. I had this and similar experiences more than once. I do not recall talking to my mother about them, but if I did, they would have been explained as dreams, and I would have been encouraged not to worry about them. Only after I started to understand projections of consciousness did I realize that these experiences were real journeys to real places that included real encounters with real people, albeit all extraphysical. Why would extraphysical consciousnesses want to attack an innocent child? Perhaps I was not so innocent after all.

My earliest memory of the specific consciousness most closely linked to me in this pathological karmic bond occurred when I was about 12 or 13 years old. I was drifting off to sleep when I suddenly felt myself kissed by cold, clammy lips that left a taste of decay in my mouth and sent a shudder through my body. I was immediately wide awake and somewhat shaken. Of course, I had no way of explaining this event and never thought of it as being a multidimensional experience. That never occurred to me as a possibility. This incident accompanied me for a while and even made me concerned about the idea of kissing girls until I forgot about it again.

The memory did not come back to me until one night, shortly after that intense energy release the first time I saw Leia, when I had another 'dream'. A woman ran at me, clutched me tightly and pulled me over a bridge. 'I will take you with me,' was her voiceless message that resonated in my mind, and the energy emanating from her was exactly the same as that childhood kiss: death, decay and coldness. As I experienced that energy, the memory of having felt it previously came flooding back.

A few days after that 'dream', which I now interpret as an extraphysical experience, I attended a Buddhist workshop on death. It was a full-day event that included classic Buddhist teachings about the impermanence of the body as well as guided meditations on the dying process. In Buddhism, the process of physical death is seen as a great opportunity to achieve heightened states of awareness. It would be exaggerated to say that I 'died', but the exercise did have a dramatic impact on me. During the first meditation that accompanied the lecture, I became increasingly uncomfortable as the monk talked us through a meditation that sought to replicate the process of dying. This involved a detailed description of the different stages experienced by consciousness: the senses becoming dimmer, the mind going inwards, and so on. My body became so uncomfortable that I felt I could not stand it any longer. As I got up to leave the room I collapsed, and my last memory was of farting as all my muscles totally relaxed. I was fully unconscious for some seconds. Whether I was able to get up and leave the room or whether I was carried out I do not remember. I was taken downstairs to recover, and soon it was lunchtime and the group had a break. I felt extremely fragile, but after the break I thought I would be up to participating again. The afternoon continued with another meditation, and within a few moments, I had fallen off my seat again. This time, I had the classic near-death experience of seeing a white light and feeling that I was flying into it. At the same time, however, I was also quite conscious of my body lying on the floor. I remained fragile for about two weeks after this occurrence. At one point, I even had to stop reading a university text that discussed a person dying from AIDS, because I began fainting as I engaged with the idea of death. It was as if the mere mention of the final bodily exit provided my psychosoma with a cue to leave.

As well as feeling fragile I also felt light, renewed and somehow deeply altered. Something had left me during that experience: the woman with whom I had been intertwined for who knows how many lifetimes. In the language of conscientiology, which I was yet to learn, the relationship I had had with this woman would be described as a form of group-karmic interprison. This means that we are in the same group of consciousnesses who share karma, and our particular relationship had been one where we were locked in a perpetrator–victim dynamic. At some point in our history, I had been the perpetrator and she the victim, but from that place of victimhood, she had become a perpetrator, acting in revenge and from a sense of being a perpetual victim. I know I started my life with this. I was highly accident-prone as a child, and by the time I was six had had numerous head injuries requiring medical assistance. I now also understand the dreams in which I was being pursued and stabbed to have been actual extraphysical projections which no doubt involved that particular consciousness but also others aligned with her and with my own negative energies. Having since learned that most children are relatively protected from intrusion that would lead to these kinds of accidents and extraphysical experiences, it is clear to me that my connection to these negative dimensions was very strong.

Love and affection can form bonds that continue across existences, but so too can hatred and anger. In this case, the interrelationship of animosity was so strong that the energies of another consciousness whom I had harmed terribly in former existences were virtually fused with mine. This means that when I was born in this lifetime, that consciousness continued to pursue me from the other side, and as my actions towards that particular consciousness date back quite a number of lifetimes, I am fairly certain that this negative relationship has influenced my intraphysical experiences more than once. Transforming such a long-term pathological relationship is perhaps most accurately described as the disentangling of the negative energetic bond between us. It is something that represents a significant shift in the evolutionary journeys of the consciousnesses involved.

In this lifetime, she was the 'negative' one, the 'intruder'. She was stuck in feelings of anger and hatred in response to my incredible cruelty of the past, and the reason we were still linked was that I had never resolved this relationship and still carried within myself the energy that had perpetuated the bond. In fact, our link had been so strong that her energies seemed to form a natural part of me. I was not able to distinguish them as coming from someone else. While my most immediate link was to this one consciousness, there was clearly a whole dimension of pathological consciousnesses with which some aspect of me vibrated in harmony. Otherwise, I would not have had projective experiences to those dimensions as a child and again later when I heard the voices from that dimension in my head. The strength of our energetic entanglements was also shown by the fact that, to be fully undone, it required the interventions of Pak Suyono, Leia and, eventually, the extraphysical helpers at the Buddhist retreat. I hope that the other party to this prison is also better off as a result of no longer being energetically locked to me.

This was perhaps the most impactful of my past-life experience, but Leia assisted me in understanding my past and the impact it was having on my present in other important ways. In 1996, I enrolled in the first interfaith seminary ever to be run in England. I felt intensely drawn to religious and spiritual ideas, and the idea of learning about all major religions and being an eclectic representative of Spirit, as I thought of it at the time, was very appealing. When I again started visiting Leia in 1997, I soon discovered why it was so appealing. Being a religious representative was what I had been doing again and again in different religions and faiths throughout my various lives. Leia either pointed things out directly, such as my Egyptian priest reincarnation, or facilitated memories. My recollection of a moment in the life of a Buddhist monk in Tibet during one of the development meetings was accompanied by an intense surge of 'his' energies that seemed to fill the entire room. Another person at the meeting who was unaware of what I was experiencing commented on a Buddhist presence. Other recollections of religious existences were less intense, but there was a Muslim mystic, a Hindu renunciate, a voodoo practitioner, and a Shinto devotee. There were other, more mundane lives too, but the religious thread was very strong. The insights into my past lives helped me understand why I was so drawn to religious ideas, and initially I did not see a problem with pursuing that path again in this life. I had little ambition other than to devote my life to some sort of spiritual purpose, and I was drawn both to the interfaith path and also to spending time in a Buddhist monastery. Once I had the powerful retrocognition of the Buddhist life, however, I started feeling uneasy with the idea. Maybe, I thought, if I had already had these experiences, I would be better off doing something else?

It was around this time, as I started to develop a sense that perhaps I was repeating myself by following a religious path yet again, that I first came across the ideas of conscientiology through its founder, Waldo Vieira. My first introduction to him was through an interview he had given in the spring 1997 edition of *Kindred Spirit Magazine* in England. And there it was: a word to describe my experience! I was in the process of repeating myself, of committing 'self-mimicry'. It is curious how being given a word for something we might have known from experience but not have been able to clearly describe can make it much more tangible. Suddenly, I understood clearly what before had been just a feeling, namely, that this 'spiritual path' that I was following so naturally was natural because it was the path I had most commonly trodden in the past. It was the path of least resistance and therefore also of least evolutionary opportunity. With this realization came the desire to not repeat it, and so, I never did become an interfaith minister or join a Buddhist monastery.

Avoidance of repetition is one good reason to seek retrocognitions. Another is the effect that past lives can have on our present manifestation. The effects of early childhood experiences are quite well understood these days. What we experience in our formative years can and will contribute enormously to our personal development. Less frequently do we consider what effects our past lives might be having on our present one. With Leia, I learned that many of our mental hang-ups are older than just our childhood. They were formed in previous lives, and are based in energy patterns that we have carried over into this life in one way or another. Once we discover this and can identify the source, we are very close to breaking the pattern. This also applies to our interpersonal relationships. Our first reactions to people, for example, are not always just based on the color of their hair or their body odor, but spring from long-forgotten relationships we have had with them. The happy or unhappy relationship you are having with your partner will not be the first time that the two of you play out the patterns that dominate your relationship now.

There were many interesting stories of the effects of multiexistentiality at Leia's meetings. One I recall was of a woman who had concerns for her son. He was suffering what had been diagnosed as some form of mental illness. He found it very difficult to assume his life in the world, and well into his twenties was still living at home and being very reclusive. Leia explained that his previous life had been spent as a woodcutter in a vast and remote forest. He had loved the lonely life and the energy of the trees, and that was where he had eventually died. The way I understood it, he had so loved that life that he was emotionally still stuck there, and although his recollections were in no way conscious, they were seriously affecting his ability to get on with life in the here and now of 20th-century England. I believe nostalgia for particularly pleasant past lives is a common phenomenon that can become a major obstacle to a successful completion of this lifetime.

The ability to recall past lives is greatly enhanced during a projection of consciousness, because in that state we can potentially access our entire memory bank. Guided meditations were a regular part of the development group at Leia's, and though they were always different, they always had the same intention of helping participants to exit their bodies. I have included one example here that you can use with one or more friends. Ideally, it is spoken in a calm and measured way by one person while the others relax:

> Sit comfortably, preferably in a chair (or lie down), with arms and legs uncrossed. Close your eyes and spend some time relaxing your body, your shoulders and back, your chest and abdomen, your arms and legs.
>
> Imagine yourself in an empty room. Feel yourself breathing.
>
> Now watch the walls. Every time you breathe in, the walls expand, and every time you breathe out, the walls contract. Watch this for a while. Now the walls are becoming still, but every time you breathe in you expand, and every time you breathe out you contract. (Allow a few moments of this.)
>
> Now you are no longer contracting. You are expanding with every in breath. You are gradually filling out the room. Now you are filling out the entire room, and with the next breath, you have become larger than the room. The room is now in you.
>
> Look up. You see the stars. You fly off towards a light you can see in the sky. On the way, you find an object. You look at it carefully and take it with you. You keep flying towards the light and discover that it is a room. You land in the room and see a number of doors. Look at them carefully and then choose the one that seems right to you. Go through the door and explore what is behind it.

At this point, the participants are left alone for some time, probably no more than 15 or 20 minutes.

This and similar guided meditations help participants to obtain a separation from their physical bodies and thereby access memories from their own integral, multidimensional memory. The guide does not provide any content about what the participants will find. This avoids suggestions that might induce false memories, one of the main risks of pursuing past-life memories through hypnosis or other techniques involving an external guide. Ideally, past-life memories will arise from within the individuals themselves and in harmony with their own evolutionary dynamic.

Chapter 9

Extraphysical Dimensions

I said earlier that Leia apparently saw physical people as moving bodies of energy. She also saw the many spirits or extraphysical consciousnesses that accompanied the people she met and spoke to. Leia was constantly engaging with extraphysical people. She might be talking to you and suddenly convey something said by someone extraphysical who was also in the room. Sometimes these extraphysical people played very important roles, at times with real physical consequences.

One story she told was of a time when one of her horses gave birth in the middle of the night. Leia had never participated in such a birth before and did not know what she had to do. She sent out a mental call for help, and a deceased veterinarian came and assisted her by talking her through the process. Another time, Leia related receiving a phone call from somebody she had never met, and as soon as she answered the phone, she was confronted by an extraphysical consciousness who had a connection to the person on the other end of the phone. While the physical person was speaking through the telephone, the extra-physical person was talking very excitedly about something she wanted Leia to communicate to her physical friend. This kind of double communication seemed to be normal for Leia. Occasionally, she would complain jokingly about the noise in her living room, indicating that the extraphysical consciousnesses were having just as lively a debate as the physical people in the room. The extraphysical population she mentioned was very varied. It ranged from members of the Boardroom to a whole host of diverse extraterrestrials from many different planets to deceased locals. Some of the interactions were friendly; others were hostile.

I accompanied Leia to a presentation once where she was scheduled to channel an extraphysical consciousness. On the way, she said that there was a tremendous queue of extraphysical people hoping they would get a chance to come through when she took the stage. Apparently, there are many more extraphysical consciousnesses with a desire to make themselves heard in our dimension than there are channels that allow them to be heard. These include channeling, Ouija boards, transcommunication, and so on. Consequently, if there is an opportunity to communicate with the physical dimension, it can lead to 'traffic jams'. At this particular event, a Ufology meeting, the consciousness being channeled was from another planet. It was also not exactly an extraphysical consciousness. Rather, it was a projector who had left his physical body back on his planet of origin and had projected in his psychosoma to communicate through Leia's body. Leia, in the meantime, visited his planet in her psychosoma.

I witnessed Leia channeling on one other occasion. During a meeting in her home, she spontaneously announced that there was a consciousness who wanted to communicate with us. What was most significant about this communication was that this consciousness said that it did not have a psychosoma but had moved past that stage and was now a free consciousness. In other words, this consciousness no longer had physical existences but manifested purely in the mental dimension using only a mentalsoma. That is the only information I recall from this brief communication, but I still clearly remember the sense of heightened exhilaration that seemed to grip the group while Leia was channeling this particular consciousness. I did not really appreciate the significance of this event at the time. It was only after proper study of multidimensional phenomena that I came to understand that if this really was a free consciousness, it would have been a very rare channeling event indeed.

As I explained in Chapter 2, the relationship between dimensions is based on energetic vibrations, and for the most part, interactions across dimensions occur between dimensions that are in closer proximity to each other in vibrational terms. For example, most people experience projections of consciousness to dimensions that are immediately adjacent to the physical dimension, and most extraphysical consciousnesses who interact with our dimension have denser energies. They either still have remains of the energetic body from their last life, or their mental and emotional pattern is still very attached to physical life. Similarly, most channelers convey communications from extraphysical consciousnesses who are from dimensions that are closer to our physical one. At times, there is a kind of relay effect where those consciousnesses relay messages from more subtle (that is, more evolved) consciousnesses. Those subtler consciousnesses are able to make themselves known to these denser extraphysical consciousnesses, perhaps also by channeling, but they can't quite make it to our physical dimension because it is energetically too difficult for them to connect with our denser frequencies.

From the perspective of conscientiology, the mental dimension of the free consciousnesses is as far removed from our physical dimension as is humanly conceivable. Many people have had glimpses of this dimension through projections in the mentalsoma (see Chapter 17 for a personal account), and they all share a struggle to express the experience of cosmic oneness that is a common feature of such projections. 'Ineffable', 'inexplicable', and 'indescribable' are some of the recurring adjectives. It is a dimension beyond time and space and truly removed from the energetic patterns and concepts of physical life. For a free consciousness to be channeled in the physical dimension would require the medium to vibrate at a very high frequency. Unlike other channelers I have seen, who have distorted voices or seem to strain when they let the extraphysical consciousness use their bodies, Leia's body was completely relaxed, and the voice was essentially hers on both occasions. It was only through the difference in energy that emanated from her that one could get a sense that there was another person involved.

It sometimes felt as though Leia was aiming specifically at getting those who came to her used to the idea that we are constantly surrounded by non-physical beings. She herself alleged to be visiting members of the development group on a regular basis in a projected state, and the more clairvoyant people in the group confirmed this. Regular attendees at Leia's meetings seemed to receive what can best be described as training sessions in multidimensional awareness from her extra-physical companions. This doesn't necessarily mean that we all became able to perceive these extraphysical people all the time, but we got used to the idea that they were around. Sometimes their presence was signaled by subtle energetic sensations such as a tingling of the ear or a wave of energy felt in the energetic body. At other times they used more physical means to make themselves known. As mentioned earlier, it was quite common for things to inexplicably go missing in people's houses, and Leia usually seemed to know what was behind these events. Another way for the extraphysical consciousnesses to make themselves known was by interfering with people's thoughts. You might suddenly find your thoughts drifting off in unusual directions, or you would come up with strange jokes that were not in line with your normal thinking. Leia had a very particular sense of humor, and the same goes for some of the extraphysical consciousnesses that surrounded her. One of their popular tricks, for example, was changing the temperature of the shower.

Another aspect of multidimensionality that became readily apparent around Leia was telepathic communication. She and her son regularly communicated telepathically, and because being at her place heightened my perception, I was sometimes privy to these interactions. Once, when Leia was telepathically asking her son to offer people cups of tea, I said, 'Yes, please', even while she was still communicating with him. It took me, and I think them, by surprise. A less successful occasion was when one of Leia's cats was, according to Leia, talking to me. The cat was clearly focused on me, but I had no idea what it was trying to communicate. As I mentioned earlier, seeing telepathy in practice made it clear to me that to Leia, as well as to many extraphysical consciousnesses, our minds are open books and that we are deluding ourselves if we think that we can keep mental secrets from the world. Someone will always know, even if they are currently extraphysical.

There is another element to telepathy that has deeper implications for our human constitution. It seems that sometimes we might be engaging in unconscious telepathic communication while we are physically communicating. Think of a scenario where you are having a polite conversation with a person at the verbal level while thinking how you really don't want to be talking to that person, or maybe even less pleasant things. What I am suggesting is that at some level these thoughts are communicated and received by the other person. Neither party may necessarily be conscious of this process, but these unspoken communications can influence our relationships more than we realize. During my interactions with Leia it quite often seemed that, while I was having one conversation with her on a verbal level, she was communicating with me quite deliberately on a telepathic level as well. I registered that this was happening, but was not always able to consciously pick up the telepathic subtext. Nonetheless, at times I had the impression that the 'unspoken' conversation later surfaced and influenced me through sudden insights or new thoughts.

Chapter 10

An Embodiment of Assistance

Leia's life and interactions, both in this and other dimensions, were essentially dedicated to assisting others. I remember, after my first meeting with her, trying to describe to somebody what her presence was like. All I could say was that she seemed to emanate pure love. This is a very rare experience, because most of our experiences of love are also accompanied by our own baggage of subconscious expectations, obligations, past hurt, mistrust and so on. Leia's presence was incredibly calming at a very deep level but also light, fun and high energy. Because I knew that I could have no mental secrets with her, I could be completely open without any fear. I felt totally accepted with all my shortcomings. This does not mean that she was always sunshine and smiles. She could have quite a stern side when she wanted to convey important information or make a point. But the underlying energy was love. During some of the meetings at her house, participants would sit on chairs while Leia would stand next to us and exteriorize, or consciously emit, energy from her hands. I found these sessions incredibly blissful, as if I were being bathed in love. They took me to a place that felt like home, and I often wished I could have just stayed there. I believe that this kind of love, by its very nature, needs to spread itself, and Leia was a channel for it to do so.

Leia lived in a state of perpetual consciousness. There was no sleeping. When her body was resting, her psychosoma traveled the world engaging in assistential work. In fact, even when her body was not resting, her energy sometimes seemed to depart. During the evening sessions at her house, it was very common for her to grow slightly vague towards the end of the evening. She explained that she was 'expected' at a certain time when she got called for duty. There was just enough of her present to maintain the body in a socially acceptable state, but the rest of her was out and about providing extraphysical assistance.

What does extraphysical assistance consist of? There are numerous ways in which one can be of assistance outside of the body. During one of these late meetings, when Leia was awake but had gone blank, I asked her what she was doing. She said that she had been called to give assistance to a small girl who was living in very precarious conditions in a city in South America. Leia had extraphysically arranged a future benefactor to meet this girl and help her out of her situation. Extraphysical minds can and do constantly affect intraphysical minds, and this is what Leia was doing in this particular instance in order to anonymously contribute to a series of intraphysical events that would impact significantly on the life of this young girl.

Another very intriguing story came from one of the people who regularly attended sessions at Leia's, a psychically very gifted young man. One day, he recounted a projection from the previous night in which he had been summoned to help, again, in an intraphysical situation. A bus driver had suffered a heart attack while driving down a mountain road with a bus full of people. This young man had taken over the bus driver's body with his psychosoma and managed to steer the bus to safety. He explained that it had felt very strange and that he had been unable to use the driver's left arm.

There are in fact many other forms of assistance, and despite all the help rendered to intraphysical consciousnesses, I have since learned that the largest amount of assistance actually occurs on the other side, that is, it is aimed at extraphysical consciousnesses. The process of 'death', or more accurately, of deactivating the physical body, is traumatic to many of us after a lifetime of believing that we are a physical body. Consequently, there is a whole structure in place to assist with the various stages of that process, including the adjustment to the other dimensions we enter after leaving the body for good. But even so, many of us do not experience a healthy death. We remain caught in physical attachments, holding on to the denser energies of the energetic body that we should really be shedding in order to be able to experience our 'new' extraphysical environment with clarity. Because of this, there are dimensions filled with millions of consciousnesses who believe they are physical and are caught in stagnant and pathological mental and emotional patterns. It is to those dimensions that many assistential efforts are devoted.

The way Leia spoke suggested that there was a certain agency that 'summoned' or 'requested' the assistance. There seem to be various levels of this. Spending time with Leia left me with no doubt that there is a definite order to the workings not only of the extraphysical dimensions but also of the intraphysical and the interaction between them. It is easy to lose sight of this amid the seeming chaos that many of us experience in our daily lives. There are individualized helpers, helpers for specific tasks or purposes, and project teams. There are helpers who specialize in working with ideas and others whose main contribution is therapeutic energy.

The Boardroom is one aspect of this multidimensional structure. It represents a group of individuals working for the benefit of all consciousnesses on this planet. Clearly the consciousnesses that work at that level are very highly evolved, and some people may wonder whether such consciousnesses still maintain individual identities. Especially in the Eastern traditions, there is often a sense that spiritual evolution means the loss of individuality and a gradual merging with an ultimate reality, such as the Buddha mind or the 'clear light'. My understanding is that the members of the Boardroom are at a significant level of evolution but that they are also still individual consciousnesses. They are, however, able to quite literally produce a meeting of minds or, better put, of mentalsomas, where they unite at a level of consciousness at which they almost act as one entity. Leia suggested that the group consciousness that is established when the Boardroom members join together in that way has a connection to all beings on this planet. She said that people sometimes have an experience of this Boardroom group consciousness and believe it to be God.

During one of her development sessions, Leia wanted to give us a taste of this merging of consciousnesses. There were perhaps six or seven of us. Leia got us all to hold hands, and then she started moving energy around the circle that we were forming. This movement of energy became increasingly intense, and as it did, I experienced a gradual loss of my sense of individual self, and simultaneously, a sense of intimate connectedness with the other participants, some of whom I did not know at all. This was accompanied by feelings of ecstasy and freedom. I am sure that this was only a pale shadow of the experience of the Boardroom, who would be joining at the level of the mentalsoma, which allows the direct transfer of entire concepts and ideas. In addition to the main Boardroom, there are 'subcommittees', regional specialists, and so on in a hierarchy that is not defined by financial gain or inherited status but by personal evolutionary conquests and the refinement of consciousness.

In conscientiology it is assumed that, on the individual level, only some of us will have our own dedicated helpers. Whether we do depends on the tasks we have set ourselves for this life, whether they are aligned with the principles of assistance and evolution and whether we are genuinely open to working with a personal helper. Sometimes one extraphysical helper may need 'backup' for a specific task and can send out a call for help to others, such as Leia, for example. If we thought of it, we in the intraphysical dimension could also put out calls for help when we feel overwhelmed by our evolutionary crises. How exactly these calls are managed and processed I do not know, but as far as I can tell, if they are genuine they are usually answered. And it is not only extraphysical helpers that respond. Many more of us intraphysical consciousnesses get involved in this type of assistance than we consciously realize. If you are a generally compassionate person and perhaps even have a sense of your ability to help others spiritually, for example, if you believe in praying for people or focusing kind and loving thoughts, chances are that you will be providing assistance of some kind outside of your body during sleep. We participate in this large multidimensional process of assistance guided by the extraphysical helpers, who will make sure that we humans attend to the job (in our psychosoma). Most of us, in our normal waking state, do not recall our nightly activities and are only vaguely, if at all, aware of these assistential roles. There are good reasons for this, which I only came to understand later, once I had studied conscientiology in Brazil (see Chapter 17). For consciousnesses like Leia, however, there is no need to dim their awareness. Her extraphysical work would have taken place with the same level of lucidity as her intraphysical work, with little or no disruption of consciousness, motivated by a love that was unconditional and would not have wavered in the face of the immense suffering found in many extraphysical dimensions, including suffering experienced by both perpetrators and victims of extreme violence perpetuated extraphysically.

In addition to this kind of assistance by way of projection, I also believe that Leia represented an energetic epicenter or focal point in the physical dimension that allowed extraphysical consciousnesses to provide assistance on a major scale. I did not fully understand the mechanism of what I was seeing at the time, but I did have certain perceptions when approaching her house. Leia's house was located in the English countryside and stood alone, surrounded by fields, on the top of a hill. I usually rode my bike to her place, and more than once when approaching her house, I had the impression of intense extraphysical activity taking place in an area extending hundreds of meters across the fields around her house. Again, I only came to fully understand these impressions once I had studied conscientiology, but I will explain this now, as it is important for understanding Leia's contribution.

Just as human energies are used for assistance during projections of consciousness, so too can they be used in this dimension to establish a space in which healthy extraphysical consciousnesses can provide assistance to sick ones. Over time, the extraphysical helpers can use the conscious regular exteriorization, or emission, of positive energies by an intraphysical consciousness to create an energetic 'bubble' where consciousnesses needing assistance can be attended. This also relates to the point I mentioned earlier, namely that it is usually only the denser extraphysical consciousnesses that interact directly with the physical dimension. It is very difficult for the more refined extraphysical helpers to engage with or spend significant amounts of time close to the physical and denser extraphysical dimensions, that is, those places where most of the assistance is needed. The energetic bubble created through the regular energetic donation by a positive intraphysical consciousness can be conceptualized as an energetic 'embassy'. This 'embassy' allows evolved consciousnesses to come close to the human dimension for extended periods in order to provide assistance to both intra- and extraphysical consciousnesses in need. The energetic bubble is referred to as an 'extraphysical office' in conscientiology. It is a space where the human being 'works' together with the helpers by making a contribution to the multidimensional process of assistance. If my perceptions were accurate, Leia's 'extraphysical office' was more like an 'extraphysical stadium'. Maintained through her intense level of energy, it seemed to provide a space where thousands of consciousnesses in need of assistance could gather at any one time.

Chapter 11

Planet Earth

As described earlier, Leia's very existence was the result of an effort by the Boardroom to transform the planet and protect it from serious damage. Leia repeatedly referred to the beauty of planet Earth as seen from space, and she described it as a rare jewel of creation that attracts consciousnesses from across our galaxy and beyond. Talking to Leia, I got the impression that what is happening on this planet in terms of the tension between destructive forces that foster war, devastation and separation and creative forces that strive for ethical living and universalism is simply a reflection of a struggle that is taking place all over the universe. One of the features that makes planet Earth special is our particular type of intraphysical dimension with the human body as a vehicle of manifestation for consciousness. This is not the only planet with an intraphysical dimension, but as a vehicle of manifestation, the human body seems to offer a very particular evolutionary environment for consciousness. Leia described human beings as an experiment gone wrong. When I once asked her to explain what she meant, she said something like: 'As always, some people went where they weren't supposed to go.' I am still no clearer on the facts, but the element of doing the forbidden is strangely reminiscent of the Adam and Eve story. The best interpretation of this statement I have so far come up with is that some consciousnesses were dabbling in making physical vehicles; that is, they wanted to make bodies that would enable them to experience intraphysical life. Maybe someone didn't follow the instructions properly and we ended up with the particular vehicle we have now, with all its limitations and short-comings.

It is hard to talk about planet Earth without talking about

extraterrestrials. Before meeting Leia I was not particularly interested in ETs and was quite happy working within the framework of the Eastern religions. Even after I had adapted to the realization that we are constantly surrounded by extraphysical people, it was yet another eye opener for me when I realized that they were not all merely 'dead' people from previous human existences but also ETs, people who until this point had never even experienced a human existence. I came to understand that the human body is only a vehicle for consciousness, just as the bodies of species from other planets are merely vehicles for consciousness. Consciousnesses can change vehicles across planets and walk in our midst looking just like us. That is probably the most common form of interplanetary travel.

The realization that extraterrestrial life exists extraphysically meant that the universe had suddenly shrunk as intergalactic communication became potentially feasible during sleep. The multidimensional nature of a lot of ET experiences is really important to keep in mind when thinking about 'abductions' and so on. I believe the consistency of the accounts, now over many decades, supports the assumption that cases of physical abduction do actually take place. Where the whole ET discussion becomes confused, however, is that it usually focuses *only* on the intraphysical and does not take other dimensions into account. Once one becomes familiar with the idea that there is an incredible number of consciousnesses in other dimensions, it seems quite ludicrous to assume that some of them should not be from other planets. I think the bar scenes in the *Star Wars* movies probably give quite a good impression of the breadth of forms in which consciousness can manifest throughout the unfathomable expanse of the multiverse. As has already become apparent, Leia gave a lot of time to UFO groups, and she clearly looked at the planet in the wider context of its role within the universe. I am confident that extraphysical extraterrestrials play a very important role in the affairs of this planet right here and now.

There is also no doubt that ETs are regularly born into their first human existence and thus suddenly become terrestrials. At some point or other, we all arrived here this way.

During my time with Leia, I had a number of experiences with ETs. One of my most conscious experiences of 'being tampered with' was at Las Pyramides on Lake Atitlán in Guatemala. I was lying on my bed, facing the ceiling and going through the B-ing meditation I had learned at Shanti Loka. I was relaxed, with my eyes closed, yet mentally alert. During this exercise, I quite commonly experience curious physical and extraphysical sensations as my consciousness expands to my energetic body and my psychosoma. Particular parts of my body might tingle, feel slightly uncomfortable or become especially energized, vibrating or pulsating. While I was lying there, I suddenly became aware through my closed eyes, that is, with my 'para-eyes', that I was surrounded by people. They fit the most common description of ETs, that of the so-called Grays. They were small with big heads and eyes and long arms, although I could not say that they were gray, as the color I saw was merely the white shimmer of energy. They were standing around me as if I was on an operating table, and one of them was injecting what appeared to be a needle into my body. Actually, it was not my physical but my energetic body, and I could feel a localized increase of energies occurring where the needle was being injected. At the same time there was a 'pricking' feeling, but it was a 'para-pricking' of the energetic body rather than of the physical skin. I have felt that pricking sensation many times since, and although I have never had such a precise vision of these particular ETs again, I am sure they have been around. I am not sure what the point of that exercise might have been, but the set-up of lying there surrounded by these guys made me feel as if I was part of some kind of experiment.

I never asked Leia about this particular experience, but she did talk about the Grays once. According to her, the Grays are a technologically extremely advanced race that got heavily into cloning technology in order to change some of their characteristics. One of their aims was to rid themselves of their emotions, as they considered them to be an obstacle. They succeeded, and only when it was too late did they realize that they had made a mistake. Without their emotions, they suffered a severely reduced quality of life. So they eventually decided to reverse the process and, drawing on their genetic technology, they decided to crossbreed with humans to achieve their aim. This is one reason for the many abduction phenomena that have been reported and popularized through books such as Whitley Strieber's *Communion*. One of the attendees at Leia's meetings expressed his disapproval at what seemed to be clearly unethical behavior, namely abducting human beings against their will and at times leaving them deeply frightened. Leia assured him that nobody was taken against his or her will and that everybody who is abducted has agreed to this taking place. The problem is that this agreement occurred prior to this lifetime, or perhaps even prior to a previous physical existence, during the intermissive period between lives. The human being here and now does not remember. As for the fear, the Grays would have no idea what that is, as understanding emotions is not their strong side.

This interaction between dimensions raises some remarkably complex issues. The principal sphere of interaction, it seems to me, between humans and Grays are the extraphysical dimensions. Many 'abductions' occur in the psychosoma, yet there are some very physical effects. In the dimension of the Grays, new children are born, and in our dimension there are women, every now and then, who claim to have had their ovaries taken from their bodies. I also have a suspicion of physical tampering occurring with some men.

There were other experiences with extraterrestrial consciousnesses, also interdimensional. I had a number of projections in which I saw flying UFOs, including one in which I was accompanied by an old friend, also projected, who unfortunately fell asleep in his psychosoma as I was trying to show him the awesome display of a fleet of spaceships moving gracefully across the sky. All of these experiences were positive in that they made me feel happy and excited. The energies of these particular ETs, of whom I only ever saw the outside of the spaceships, were definitely 'good' or, perhaps more objectively, these ETs operated at high energetic frequencies that equate to energies we humans experience as joy or even euphoria.

I also experienced ETs connecting themselves to my energy field while wide awake in my physical body. I have already described the energetic body that vitalizes our physical bodies. This energetic body goes slightly beyond the physical body by about one to two centimeters, but our entire energetic field is larger than that. It includes what people sometimes refer to as the 'aura', though it extends even beyond that. In conscientiology this personal energetic space is called the 'psychosphere'. It could essentially be imagined as that area around us that is most defined by our thoughts and emotions. It is also an area in which we, as we develop our sensitivities, can most readily perceive the energies of others.

During my waking state, I once spent several hours with someone who was extraphysical, and definitely not human, coupled to my energetic body. I had gone into a deep meditation in the morning, and for some reason when I finished I had this non-human person linked to me. I do not recall projecting during the meditation, but I assume that I left the body and brought this person back with me from another dimension. For whatever reason, he then attached himself to my energetic sphere.

Unfortunately, I did not have enough awareness to under-stand who this person was or why he had linked himself to me, but he was very tangible in my energetic field. He was humanoid, but very broadly built and there seemed to be strips dangling down from him, as if his clothes were torn and ragged;

only I think those strips were part of his body. And I wasn't the only one who could sense his energy. As I was going for a walk on the beach, feeling highly conscious of the unusual energies in my personal sphere, 'I' set off a dog whose path I crossed. The owner seemed surprised at the dog's angry reaction, but it was clear to me that the dog was reacting to the strange energies of the ET that seemed to be coming from me. Later I learned about a case in which Waldo Vieira had spent several years with an extraterrestrial consciousness attached to his psychosphere to assist him in the process of adapting to the energies and attributes of the human body before assuming his first life on Earth. Perhaps in my case the consciousness was just having an initial look around and was using me for the visit due to some energetic compatibility in my energy field.

So far I have spent this chapter about planet Earth largely talking about ETs, which makes sense once we understand that all consciousnesses on this planet originally came from somewhere else. But the planet itself is an incredible creation and a consciousness in its own right. I already mentioned that Leia called her Sophia. And just as the human body is composed of numerous fields and centers of energy, so is Sophia's body, our planet Earth.

According to Leia, the planet has seven primary energetic centers that are marked by seven crystals deep inside the Earth. Or perhaps the crystals are actually extraphysical and located in other dimensions, but if so, they nonetheless have a very real relationship with the geography of the planet. Each of these crystals is associated with a particular color, the principal two being black and white. Somewhat predictably, the black crystal is associated with negative energy and the white one with positive. The black one is apparently located in the Middle East. The violent history of that area might to a large extent be due to this fact. The white crystal is apparently off the coast of Burma, an area that has also known its share of suffering.

Leia said that the Boardroom had quite recently (in 1996) taken the unprecedented step of attempting to shut down the black crystal. A cover was placed around it so that no new energy could get through. She compared the effect of this measure with that of starving a flame of oxygen. Eventually, it will suffocate itself. However, before it does so, it might thrash wildly. Again, it is important to remember the multidimensional nature of existence when thinking about this. Maybe there are physical crystals in these places, and maybe these are also important, but my understanding is that the essentials are taking place in other dimensions.

If this idea seems fanciful to you (I know it did to me), I would invite you to try to connect with the energy of the white crystal. Depending on what works for you, you may do so during a meditation, but you could also simply try to establish an energetic link with it in your normal waking state. One of the things about the subtle energies of our energosoma is that they are not bound by space and time, at least not in the same way as physical matter. You can be sitting in your living room and tune into energy anywhere on the planet. Depending on the type of sensitivity that you have, you may perceive the energy you tune into as bodily sensations, smells or shifts in your own energetic body. During the twelve months or so that I had some association with Leia, I would regularly seek to connect with that crystal as a source of energy. My intention was to channel its energy into my environment for the benefit of those around me. I am certain that I was tapping into something real, because I could feel the energy, and at times it seemed to be having an uplifting effect on the people in my vicinity.

The only other crystal that I am quite confident about is a green one located at Iguassu Falls, in the border region of Brazil, Argentina and Paraguay. Leia did not give me this detail, but my own experiences during projections of consciousness led me to this conclusion. These experiences relate directly to my time of study with Waldo Vieira. I also have a few ideas about some of the other four crystals, but nothing I would be prepared to commit to at this stage.

There are certain consciousnesses linked to these crystals that seem to function as extraphysical guardians. The white crystal, for example, is associated with a black panther or jaguar. Leia was the first to talk about this consciousness. Then there were reports in my local area of Kent that a large black wild cat had been sighted. When somebody asked Leia about this, she explained that it was actually the black panther of the crystal. He is extraphysical, but sometimes people have glimpses of other dimensions. The reason he was 'prowling' the English countryside is that he is continuously following the energy lines that traverse the planet and for which the crystals are the centers in a similar way that the chakras are centers for the energetic meridians of the human body. I became quite convinced of the existence of this particular creature some time later. While I was studying conscientiology in Brazil, one of the instructors mentioned that their organization had an extraphysical helper in the form of a black panther. For me, there was no coincidence there.

In addition to these natural features of the planet's energetic system, human activities also leave energetic imprints on a significant scale. Leia once said that one of the features that most stands out from space to clairvoyants like her is Mount Kailash. Of course, the way Leia visits outer space is by projecting outside of her physical body, and the things that stand out to her are not physical structures (such as the Great Wall of China, which is apparently visible from outer space) but energetic phenomena. Mount Kailash in the Himalayas is a holy mountain for all the religions of the region: Hinduism, Buddhism, Bon and others. It has been the object of fervent prayer and ceremonies for thousands of years. Leia said that the mountain is surrounded by a whirl of energy that rises several kilometers into the sky. No doubt there are other energetic imprints in the world that are less benign than that!

Chapter 12

Leia's Impact on My Journey

In this chapter I will pull together some of the experiences I had during the twelve months or so that I occasionally met Leia. There were some experiences that she facilitated directly, such as the time when she helped me regain awareness outside of my body and took me beyond the limits of Earth's atmosphere into space. Most of the experiences, however, did not happen while she was present as such, but I think that her energies provided a catalyst for dredging up a lot of my own energetic past. In hindsight, the time during which I was associated with her seems like one long peak experience.

Peak Experiences

So-called 'peak experiences' or remarkable states of consciousness are a common feature of the journey to greater consciousness for many who start meditating, working with energy or pursuing projections of consciousness. In my own case, these experiences have included visions of other dimensions; cosmic consciousness; projections of consciousness to various types of environments, from the most negative to the sublime; visual, auditory and tactile perceptions of extraphysical consciousnesses; a multitude of energetic phenomena; and both retrocognitions and precognitions. As mentioned previously, the Eastern traditions, Buddhism in particular, usually teach that these kinds of experiences are just as illusory as physical life, and they advise people not to become attached to them. While I agree in principle that extraphysical experiences and dimensions are no more 'real' than physical ones, I still find this approach is unsatisfactory. I think that there is much to be learned from exploring such experiences of consciousness, both about ourselves and about the nature of reality and I look forward to a time when they are commonplace and shared freely among people. But I also think that it is important not to overvalue experiences for their own sake.

A person can be a regular conscious projector and nonetheless be an immature human being or misuse psychic power to manipulate others for personal gain. My own experiences of cosmic consciousness provided me with deep insights into the nature of my own self, but they did not help me directly with key questions related to everyday living, such as how to parent my children, make real estate decisions or determine my professional career. The fact that psychic experiences may not directly assist us with such decisions does not mean that they are not intrinsically valuable. I have gained peace, motivation and direction from a lot of my experiences. But they can also become a distraction and at worst lead to alienation from the physical responsibilities we have all assumed by taking on our current physical body. On the other hand, the process of clearing old and obsolete energy patterns, reconfiguring our own thoughts and emotions and repaying karmic debts can involve intense and, from an evolutionary perspective, necessary peak experiences.

As you will recall, I initially had significant resistance, both to traveling to Shanti Loka and afterwards to meeting Leia. I think my resistance was in response to the changes I subconsciously knew would occur if I took the next step. Once I started spending time with Leia, I realized that at some level I had already known I would meet her. Even before I visited Shanti Loka, I had experienced a feeling of expectation, a sense that someone would come into my life who would make a big impact. Our encounter was an important part of my own energetic healing and I am certain that either it had been planned prior to my current resoma, or I had experienced precognitive projections about it in this life. Such projections, where we see glimpses of the future, are more common than we often realize. Most of the time we do not actively remember them, but their impact surfaces as hunches, or déjà vu experiences, or a sense of 'being on the right track'. At some stage things were lined up extraphysically for me to meet Leia in the physical dimension. It was a crucial encounter for the direction of my life. My brief time with her provided me with an energetic boost and a broadening of the mind. It ensured that I did not get stuck on what for me was the familiar path of Buddhism and instead set me on track for the much more productive evolutionary endeavors that were to follow.

Retrocognitions

Earlier, I briefly referred to the phenomenon of retrocognition and its important role in helping us to understand the influence of our own past on our decisions and relationships today. I experienced retrocognitions in several different ways: spontaneously during my waking state; through deliberate energetic interventions by Leia; and during projections of consciousness. All of these experiences shared a profound energetic charge that clearly distinguished them from either dreams or daydreams.

As briefly mentioned earlier, it was Leia who facilitated the experience that helped me finally understand that life in a Buddhist monastery would have amounted to self-mimicry. This happened during one of her development group meetings, where participants were paired up and given the task of picking up past-life information from each other. My partner did not really seem to be getting anything from me when Leia suddenly butted in and started describing me as a Tibetan monk arriving at a monastery one winter's night. As she spoke, I suddenly seemed to be seeing through the eyes of the monk, and it was as if an energetic door had opened and the energies of this particular person ('me') were right there with us, emanating from me. Shortly afterwards, one of the people from another pair thought she was picking up on a Buddhist life from her partner until Leia pointed out that her impressions were caused by the energies coming from me, which were interfering with others in the room.

Experiencing a retrocognition on the basis of information provided by another about our past lives is not ideal under normal circumstances. It is better and more reliable for such memories to emerge from ourselves. In this case, however, I completely accept the account because it came with a very powerful and personal energetic charge that I carried for some hours after the meeting. I could smell the snow and through the eyes of the monk see aspects of the experience that Leia was not describing. That past-life experience also made perfect sense of my tendencies and considerations in this life at that time.

Other subtler experiences arose during my regular daily life. Some retrocognitions were not single memories but arose as perceptions in my body that could persist for several days. Sometimes they were triggered by my trying to understand particular character traits. For example, I had adopted a vegetarian diet shortly after my return from Shanti Loka in response to my strong inner perception of meat as a dead creature. But once I started spending time with Leia, I went through a period where I experienced a sense of guilt about eating at all. I became very skinny, and felt conflicted and quite confused about my relationship towards food. Eventually, I focused my mind on trying to work out what was going on. I still recall standing in the kitchen of my house when I suddenly felt a memory arising from within my body. It was a memory of a previous body of mine, that of an ascetic monk in India. It was incredibly skinny, and the person ('me') felt great pride in his 'spiritual' discipline of having mastered the body, which in that context was considered shameful and something to be overcome. I was able to tune into that memory for several days, and once it had arisen, I felt much more relaxed about food again. I understood that the body is an important vehicle for me in this lifetime and that I do not need to fight or overcome its urges to live a spiritual life. But I did need to release the energy of that previous lifetime to be free of its psychological and emotional influences.

In a similar experience, again through a bodily memory, I recalled a life as a Japanese woman who suffered from extreme loneliness, anger and resentment in her position as a live-in servant to wealthy but highly controlling aristocrats. Again, these emotions had arisen in my daily life, seemingly irrationally, and they again eased with the appreciation of their source.

I have also experienced retrocognitions in the course of projective experiences during regular nightly sleep. Most were spontaneous, but one arose during the night after I had unsuccessfully tried to induce it through a regression technique. The technique had been applied at Las Pyramides in Guatemala, and it involved hyperventilation to produce an altered state of consciousness. Participants were then talked through a process that was designed to take our memories back to certain moments in time. I can recall there being three separate stages: early childhood, birth, and finally the period before birth. The purpose of this last stage was not to connect us to memories of our extra-physical life immediately before birth, but with a previous lifetime. I lost consciousness ('slept') during that final exercise. That night, however, I projected, and a movie played out before me in which I was an African woman engaged in some very disturbing ritualistic processes in an attempt to harness 'spiritual power'. That particular life episode was very unpleasant, and I understood why my mind might have wanted to introduce this memory in a more detached way rather than through the intense recall I could have had during the group exercise.

Finally, I have had a range of retrocognitive experiences that were triggered in one way or another by other people during my daily life. When I say 'triggered', I do not mean that they were triggered in the same way that Leia actively triggered experiences in others but unconsciously, simply from meeting certain people again.

Once we start fully appreciating the impact of our past lives on our current existence, we realize that very few of our relationships are with new people. We have had previous encounters with almost everybody with whom we now have relationships of any intensity. I have come to recognize the benefit of paying close attention at first meetings with people, to try to discern the energies of those first encounters. In doing so, I have noticed a similar pattern, what I would describe as a 'flash of recognition' in the faces of some people with whom I subsequently had very difficult relationships. I believe that those difficulties were of some antiquity and that the flash of recognition arose in response to the very strong emotional content of our relationship, unconscious to us at that moment but nonetheless present and with real effects. More positive memories have arisen in the course of having sex with lovers. One especially intense memory of that sort involved suddenly and very tangibly perceiving my partner as the male and myself as the female. The point is that past lives have a very real impact, and although their influence may seem subtle, they actually affect all areas of our manifestation and interactions.

As should be clear by now, there are many benefits to retrocognitive experiences. They can arise as a natural manifestation of our personal evolution as we move through different phases in our psychological and mental processes that are linked to specific past lives. The recollections in those cases are linked to an energetic release that allows us more freedom in our personal manifestation from that point on. They can provide us with an understanding of our strengths and weaknesses and help us make decisions that are most congruent with the evolutionary journey of our consciousness, avoiding unnecessary repetitions. They can also expand our sense of universalism, of feeling connected with consciousness in all its forms and deepening our empathy and compassion, as we realize that we have all been the victim and the perpetrator, the saint and the sinner, as well as members of the opposite sex and all other races (including extraterrestrial).

Cosmic Consciousness

Another significant experience I had during this time was what is sometimes called a 'cosmic consciousness' experience. I use the term 'cosmic consciousness' to refer to a state of consciousness where I felt detached from my physical body but connected to the whole cosmos and at times even as if I *were* the whole cosmos. I experienced this type of state a number of times, though there were variations in the way it manifested. On some occasions, it was almost purely blissful with only a slight hint of anxiety at the loss of 'self' towards the latter part of the experience. On other occasions, there was a somewhat higher degree of anxiety at the sense that my identity was disintegrating. As with many of my other experiences, I later learned that there is quite a bit of literature on this experience, and I now understand it to be caused by a complete or partial projection of the consciousness in the mentalsoma. But I did not know this when I had it.

The first of these experiences was induced while practicing *zazen*, the seated meditation posture of Zen Buddhism, in my bedroom in Kent. While sitting and being aware of my posture and my breath, I suddenly perceived a surge of energy from my abdominal area upwards that was accompanied by a cracking sound. I actually felt quite nauseous and lay down shortly afterwards. The next thing I experienced was a sense of energy lifting off the top of my head, which felt as if it had opened to the sky and the depth of the cosmos. Visions of distant galaxies and beautiful dimensions unfolded before my inner eye and I was overcome by the knowledge that my life, all life, was a perfect manifestation of the same energy that united this vast, complex and beautiful system. Energy seemed to be pouring out of me, and I felt connected to everything. All the chattering voices that normally occupied my mind were silent while I sat and watched in awe the vista of perfection that unfolded before my mental eye. I am unsure how long this lasted or exactly what I did. I know that after some time I felt I could not contain the experience in my room. It was too large! So I went and sat by the sea out the back of my house. There I had the vision of the Jesus figure walking on water that I described earlier. Then I felt that I could not keep this experience to myself, that I needed to share it somehow, so I went and visited a university friend. I still felt as if blissful energy was pouring out of me everywhere, but he did not seem to notice. Slowly some of my voices started coming back as I began to be self-conscious and inhibited about sharing my experience. Over the next few hours, I gradually returned to a more habitual state of consciousness.

I later came to understand that the experience had involved the arousal of what in the Indian traditions is called *kundalini* energy. This is the energy that moves through the central channel of our energetic system from our base or root chakra, situated at the base of the spine, to the crown chakra at the apex of the skull. The rising of this kundalini energy seems to relate to an awakening of the wider energetic system of chakras, resulting in an expansion of consciousness through a full or partial projection of the mentalsoma. For two or three weeks after arousing this energy, similar but much briefer states of consciousness arose on a number of occasions during meditation. I would sit down to practice the B-ing meditation, and within seconds it felt as if the top of my head had been opened up again and that I was connected to the cosmos. It was both blissful and slightly overwhelming because the energy felt too strong for me to contain. On one occasion, I entered this state spontaneously while at the supermarket. I felt very self-conscious, because I again felt unable to contain this cosmic energy, and it seemed as if people would notice. Of course, they did not, and there was a distinct irony in the situation: I felt like the living embodiment of the cosmos, and I was embarrassed about it!

Awakening the kundalini energy is an important step in the development of any consciousness during each new physical lifetime. It relates to a fully functioning energetic body in which all our chakras are able to move freely and the energies of the 'lower' chakras are integrated with those of the 'higher' ones. I don't think it has to be as dramatic as my experience. The energies can start flowing upward more gradually. But at some point during the process of awakening to our multidimensional energetic reality, many people go through a crisis experience in which their sense of self is rattled and the identity they have had until that time comes into question through the perception of a different identity that sits beyond the self-defining chatter of the mind. The state of cosmic consciousness is a state of consciousness that comes and goes. Like any other state, it does not define the individual. It does not signify that the person is now more evolved or forever transformed. It is ephemeral, but it can provide an experiential focal point and a particularly powerful perspective on our timeless and immortal nature.

Extraphysical Companions

I have already alluded to the presence of extraphysical consciousnesses that assumed something akin to coaching roles for those attending Leia's meetings. One of the things I believe they were trying to help us learn was that there are extraphysical consciousnesses around us all the time. Most of these, however, do not interact with us as 'coaches' but vary from indifferent to mischievous to malign. A memorable interaction with one such consciousness occurred while I was cycling through a forest near Canterbury on a sunny autumn day. I stopped to inspect a dead rabbit that was lying under a tree. I could not make out why it had died as it was young and seemed unharmed. As I stood up from a crouched position I became lightheaded, then actually lost consciousness for a few seconds and fell over. I was a bit shaken as I got up and also had the feeling that I had not fallen over by myself but that someone else was present and had interfered with me. I got back on my bike, and as I started to ride there was a loud thumping and crunching sound right next to me, as if something quite large was stomping through the autumn leaves that covered the ground. I could not see anything, but I could clearly tell where the invisible something was from the thumping sound which traveled next to me for a few meters and then veered off into the forest. I still have no idea what this presence was, but it was not very friendly.

Other consciousnesses were friendlier and more subtle. I am not overly psychic and have only clearly seen extraphysical consciousnesses on a few occasions. Most of the time, I became aware of different energies that seemed to touch me in some way, often around the ears and head. At other times I would feel it more on a whole-body level through my energetic body. On yet other occasions, I would notice my feelings and thoughts changing in unusual directions, and I would realize that someone was feeling or thinking 'through me'.

One of the lessons from the intruder with whom I had been entwined at the beginning of this lifetime was a practical demonstration of how our extraphysical company can determine our sense of 'who we are'. In other words, we tend to think of ourselves as a particular individual, when we may in fact be expressing many traits that are actually those of our extraphysical companions, for better or for worse. This becomes only really apparent, however, when those companions have moved on and we suddenly feel different. In a more positive manner, this happened to me again when I met a new helper the day I first made contact with the International Institute of Projectiology and Conscientiology, the research organization founded by Waldo Vieira. I describe this event in the next chapter.

The key point to understand is that we are all surrounded by extraphysical people all the time and that they interact with us more often than we realize. Developing our own energetic and psychic capacity means that we can take greater charge of these interactions. Rather than allowing ourselves to be the unconscious playthings of extraphysical consciousnesses, we can take the energetic initiative, making our interactions deliberate and focused on assistance.

Projections of Consciousness

Projections of consciousness were an important part of Leia's life, and there were a few times when I became aware that she assisted me in leaving the body as well as gaining some level of consciousness outside of it and maintaining some recall afterwards. In one memorable experience I briefly mentioned earlier, she took me beyond the Earth's atmosphere into space. My overwhelming memory is of being among the stars and of being immersed in Leia's energies, which made me feel ecstatic, a feeling that lingered upon my return to the body.

That period of my life was ideal for exploring this aspect of reality. I was a single university student with no other responsibilities and there was nothing to stop me from lying down in the middle of the day to try to leave my body. During this period, I was only ever what I would call semi-successful at this. I did experience myself outside of my body on a number of occasions, but there were always limits to my level of awareness.

I had a series of experiences where I remained aware of my physical body while also being aware of a part of myself that seemed to be flying about and experiencing things. The perceptions of that part were very real and seemingly independent of the physical part. For example, I was lying on my bed, conscious of my physical body, but I was also conscious of flying above and at times through the houses in my area, until I decided to visit a friend's house. At his place, I saw the physical people sitting around the kitchen table at the time, and I also perceived some extraphysical people standing around them in the kitchen. These experiences of double awareness were confusing. The fact that I continued to perceive my physical body made me question the reality of the subtle perceptions I was having at the same time. It was only during sleep that I seemed to experience the full out-of-body state where the physical body did not feature. On one such occasion, I found myself whispering into a friend's ear something I had wanted to communicate to her during the day but had not felt able to do so for fear of being misunderstood. My daytime desire had been translated into extraphysical action. I then glided back to my body, which was lying on my bed, and woke up upon entering it. On another occasion, I found myself hovering directly above my physical body but unable to move away from it. It was as if I were stuck to an energetic cord that seemed to be coming from my chest. Gradually, I became concerned, and the irrational fear arose in my mind: what if my body died with me stuck here? When I finally re-entered my body, I found it was ice-cold.

Most of the time, my sense of being projected was largely due to the energetic sensations I had *afterwards*. I would wake up buzzing with energy. Or when I got up to go to the bathroom, I would find that I did not seem to be properly in my body because I would see energetic outlines around objects and notice a delay between my feet hitting the ground and feeling the expected sensation. Sometimes upon awakening, I would experience energetic showers, that is, the sensation of having energies pour over me. But because of the lack of recall of the extraphysical perceptions and events from the actual projected period, accepting the connection between these sensations and the projections of consciousness that I intuited myself to be having took me a long time. My mind kept questioning whether maybe I was just imagining things, yet I could not deny the very real energetic sensations, which included tingling, pulsating, vibrating and the very distinct activation of chakras. I also felt exalted and energized after these experiences.

Energetic Sensitivity

As I have previously described, one of the effects of the psychic opening that happened to me at Shanti Loka was that I became highly sensitive to other people's energies. I found going to crowded places very difficult because I would get mentally and physically agitated. I didn't really understand this sensitivity at the time, but I now know that I was absorbing and being influenced by the energies of the physical people and their non-physical companions. It is an impact that many sensitive and psychic people experience. For some it can be almost debilitating, because it limits their ability to visit cities and other places with large accumulations of people.

The effect that Leia had on me over a number of visits was a gradual building up of my energetic defenses. I recall a visit to London towards the end of my association with her where I could literally feel the energetic barrier between me and the crowds around me. It was a very novel experience, because prior to that I had always felt the need to keep my visits to the big city as brief as possible. I often preferred to walk rather than catch the tube and be stuck with people at close proximity, and I would flee home as soon as my business was finished. This time I actually enjoyed spending time around Piccadilly Circus, watching the goings-on and experiencing the energies without being thrown into emotional turmoil by them. I was conscious, though, that these defenses were borrowed, the result of having received regular energy boosts from Leia. But I would soon get to develop my own defenses when I moved to Rio de Janeiro.

Chapter 13

Moving On

It was the spring of 1997, my time at university was coming to an end, and I needed to decide what I would do next. It was clear to me that my priority was a 'spiritual life', though in hindsight, I realize that I had an immature and somewhat alienated approach to life and what it meant to make 'spirituality' my priority. Given the opportunity, I would have spent most of my time in meditation or in pursuit of extraphysical experiences. When I wasn't doing that, I was a space cadet, with my head in other dimensions and real difficulties managing my day-to-day inter-personal relationships. I did not have any conventional ambitions. I was not interested in postgraduate studies at the time, and the only reason I wanted a job was for its survival value, not because I was interested in a career of any description. With the 'Buddhist monk career' now made obsolete through the new insights gained from my recent retrocognitions, I was afloat. Where to direct my spiritual drive?

Signposts soon emerged. One day, I went into a local health-food store that I did not normally frequent to buy coffee, something I had actually decided no longer to drink. The point here is that I had stepped outside my usual routine, probably under the guidance of extraphysical helpers whom I was unable to perceive directly. As I was standing at the counter, my eyes fell on a magazine called *Kindred Spirit*. I had never previously bought a copy of this publication, but that day the picture of a white-domed building on the cover caught my attention. I had actually seen this building during a semi-conscious projection not long before! I immediately grabbed the magazine, and in it I found an interview with the Brazilian medical doctor Waldo Vieira, whom the magazine billed as the 'Multidimensional Man'.

I was completely captivated. In a few short pages, Waldo gave names to a range of experiences I had been having. Most significantly for me at this point was his use of the term 'self-mimicry' that I discussed previously. But I also related very much to his account of providing energetic assistance to others around him. That was what I thought I had been doing for some time, but I had felt unsure about it and thought that maybe I was just imagining it. Here the concept was being normalized. Other experiences he described I could not personally relate to. For example, his account of a projection during which he met a recently deceased friend who did not realize that he was no longer physical. To demonstrate to his friend, Waldo took apart his own psychosoma, thereby making the point that his physical shape did not limit him in that extraphysical state. I understood what he was saying, but I had never experienced anything like it and did not have recollections of extraphysical conversations at that level of detail. In addition to his ideas, Waldo talked about the organization he had founded, the International Institute of Projectiology and Conscientiology (IIPC). 'Projectiology' was his term for the study of the projection of consciousness, while 'conscientiology' referred to the broader study of consciousness.

Could this be my new direction? Might the IIPC be my spiritual home for this lifetime? A week or two after I read this article, Leia took us through a visualization technique during one of her development sessions in order to induce a projection. This time the focus was on flying high above the planet and, while looking down, identifying some of the crystals Leia had said were embedded in it. My attention spontaneously went to South America, where I identified what I thought was a green crystal in the area of Iguassu Falls, the site of the white-domed buildings of Waldo Vieira's organization. I shot down towards it like lightning, 'hugging' it and merging with its energy, which had me tingling and buzzing all over, including after I returned to my physical consciousness. It was clear. I was going to Brazil!

I felt euphoric with the clarity of this new direction and subsequently had a range of projections that took me to Brazil.

I still had to finish my final exams, but in the meantime I planned on attending some workshops that were being run by IIPC instructors who were visiting the UK. So I headed to the Golden Square Bookshop in London one Saturday morning to attend workshops given by Wagner Alegretti and Nanci Trivellato, two experienced conscientiology instructors. The workshops themselves were very different from anything I had ever done before in terms of the clarity and frankness with which multidimensional phenomena were discussed. But the most significant experience for me occurred outside of the workshops. As I waited in the square for which the bookshop was named, I watched as a group of people congregated, also clearly waiting to enter the shop. They seemed like a close-knit group, many embracing each other or exchanging warm handshakes. At this stage, I had spent more than a year feeling somewhat alone on my spiritual journey, and here were what I thought would be my new fellow travelers. As I sat by myself thinking about this and feeling very optimistic about this new chapter of my life, I suddenly became aware of a strong energetic extraphysical presence that appeared in front of me. He semi-materialized with a distinct outline but blurry detail. 'I have been waiting for you' resounded in my mind, as a strong energetic charge hit me straight in the solar plexus. I felt mildly euphoric after this energetic exchange, which I think was initiated by a new helper who stepped into my life as I moved into this new direction.

Shortly afterwards people started to file into the bookshop, and I followed along, moving with the group of 20 or so who had been gathering outside. On entering the room, I quickly noticed that this was not the right group. The IIPC event was being held upstairs. So up I went, and the contrast could not have been starker. The welcome was friendly enough, but there was only a handful of people and no hugs or warm handshakes. Instead, the focus was on facts and rationality. I listened and found it interesting, but at that stage those workshops were all but irrelevant. I had made up my mind and was heading to Brazil as soon as I finished my exams.

It turned out that my desire for congeniality would not be met as I had hoped in Brazil, either. The evolutionary dynamic required was more rigorous than warm handshakes and hugs. There was no doubt that I was heading off to join many old evolutionary colleagues. But for some of us, our last physical encounters had perhaps not been entirely positive, and this surfaced anew in some of our energetic exchanges. One of the great benefits of the series of physical lifetimes through which we move is that it provides us with opportunities to reconnect with others again and again until we heal our relationships and transform them from cycles of mutual retribution into assistential partnerships. There is no better place to do this than in an organization that focuses on the multidimensional levels of existence and that challenges those who get involved to be frank with their energetic, emotional and intellectual reality in relation to others. So while my new group of evolutionary colleagues may not have looked exactly as I wanted, it was exactly what I needed!

Before going into more detail about my time in Brazil, I have to take a brief detour to one of the most important events of my life. In December 1996, I traveled to Australia to spend Christmas with my paternal family in Adelaide. During this time, I reignited a relationship with a young woman I had last met during a visit four years earlier. She is now my wife, but at that particular time, a relationship was the last thing on my mind. That did not stop our first child from being conceived! I was in no way ready to assume any kind of relationship responsibilities, let alone those of a parent. Despite my sexual desires, I was utterly detached from the woman and the fact that I was going to have a child. In hindsight, my attitude seems incredibly immature, and from one perspective, the fact that I pursued my spiritual journey in Brazil while my son was being born in Australia could be interpreted as selfish or irresponsible. But I do not think I would have been ready to be a partner and a father without the experiences I was going to have in Brazil. They helped me mature to a point where I had much greater integration between my physical and extraphysical life. Today, my family is a fundamental part of my evolutionary journey and a rich source of both growth-enhancing challenges and support. I would never have guessed this when I boarded the plane for Brazil in 1997.

PART 4

REASSEMBLING THE PIECES

Chapter 14

Waldo Vieira, the IIPC and Rio de Janeiro

This section of the book is a bit different from the approach taken so far. Pak Suyono and Leia were teachers, but they provided ad hoc and very personalized information. Waldo Vieira, on the other hand, as well as being psychic and energetically gifted, is an academic and a professional educator. He has written many books and developed an entire system for understanding consciousness. He also had a personal impact on me, but it was really the system of study and understanding that he developed that helped me put all my experiences together. The system he teaches is called conscientiology, and while I learned it from him and through his books, conscientiology itself is independent of him, and I also learned from the many other conscientiology instructors and students I met in Brazil. I will still be drawing on personal experiences in this section, but I also start drawing ideas together and explaining the processes I have been involved in ever since I visited Shanti Loka.

As I traveled to Rio de Janeiro, I had the feeling that I was on a mission. Visions, projections and synchronicities all seemed to be guiding me, and I was sure that I was finally going to connect with my spiritual community. I felt certain that, one way or another, I would end up at Iguassu Falls, the place I had projected to repeatedly and the site where conscientiology's first campus was being constructed. Little did I know that I would spend a year in Rio de Janeiro, an overcrowded, polluted, poverty-stricken and crime-ridden metropolis. A place I would have found completely intolerable only a few months earlier. But now, thanks to a full tank of energy from Leia, I managed the energetic intensity fairly well. I caught a bus from the airport with a few other foreigners, one of whom suggested we share an apartment. It seemed pretty clear to me, however, that his intentions were focused on sexual adventures rather than on explorations of consciousness, so I politely declined and found myself a hostel. As I settled into my bunk bed on my first night, I experienced an energetic drill-like sensation penetrating my temple. It seemed to be coming from a presence in the middle of the room. It was followed by a deep sleep state and a very joyous projection involving a spaceship. I felt I had been welcomed. The very next day, I made my way to the main office of the IIPC, located at that time in the beachfront suburb of Ipanema.

The IIPC

The International Institute of Projectiology and Conscientiology was founded in 1988, two years after the publication of Waldo Vieira's landmark treatise *Projectiology: Panorama of Experiences of the Consciousness Outside the Human Body*. The purpose of the IIPC is to provide a structure for both teaching and further developing the study of consciousness. It is a not-for-profit organization run by volunteers from all walks of life, who come to the organization because they feel a strong affinity for its approach to understanding consciousness: scientific, non-dogmatic, experiential and multidimensional. In Brazil, the IIPC is a substantial organization with representatives in most major towns and cities. Some of the younger people who come to it actually recall preparing themselves during their last intermissive period to work in the field of conscientiology. My perspective on the organization is essentially limited to the group of people who worked at the headquarters in Ipanema. They were a highly dedicated team, mostly from professional backgrounds, who devoted a substantial part of their lives to running the administrative, marketing, financial and educational programs and responsibilities of the organization.

Since that time, a great number of organizations researching specific aspects of conscientiology have sprung up. Outside of

Brazil, conscientiology is now taught through a group called the International Academy of Consciousness, and it is with that organization that I am currently volunteering in Australia. But I knew nothing about any of this when I first walked through the doors of the IIPC in 1997.

Waldo Vieira

As coincidence would have it, Antonio Pitaguari, the man in charge of the IIPC's London office at the time, had just come back to Rio for a visit. Not only did he take me through the first few classes of the IIPC's curriculum, but he also accompanied me on my first visit with Waldo Vieira, to whom he introduced me in the IIPC boardroom.

Waldo is an imposing presence, tall, invariably dressed in white with a bald crown surrounded by a large mane of white hair, and a long white beard. His energetic presence is even more striking than his physical appearance. He is enthusiastic and expressive, and his intense eyes seem to look right to one's core. As I entered, Waldo was drinking a can of coke, which was not what I expected of a spiritually enlightened person. I was a vegetarian at the time and quite skinny, and I recall this initial conversation focusing on whether I would eat meat. There are many unconventional aspects to Waldo, and his views on eating certainly clashed with the ideals of most Eastern spiritual practices. For Waldo, meat is not only an essential ingredient for human well-being; its dense energies also play an important role in our ability to be of assistance in other dimensions.

At that point in my life, I had circulatory issues and frequently experienced ice-cold hands. During this first conversation, Waldo suddenly reached out and grabbed both my hands, saying, 'You will overcome this.' As soon as he touched my hands they became warm and tingly, but it took another ten years or so, and a change in diet, for me to really overcome that particular issue. Apart from these details, the main thing I recall from my first encounter with Waldo was his warm enthusiasm and the overwhelming sense that he was 100 percent committed to the tasks he had set himself in this lifetime: to develop a greater understanding of our multidimensional nature and to make that understanding available to as many people as possible.

Apart from our introductory meeting, I rarely had personal time with Waldo. I don't know whether he even did any work with smaller groups of people. I would see him in the IIPC offices, where he spent most of his time in the boardroom that he, as president of the IIPC, occupied with its three directors. He would usually say a congenial greeting when coming and going, and occasionally he would stop for a chat with one person or another, but I had little direct contact apart from the odd encounter along the corridor or in the kitchen. When I did bump into him, I was usually very nervous. On those occasions, Waldo often seemed to look with great intensity not at me but at the space around my head. I knew that he was incredibly clair-voyant. I had seen him confuse an extraphysical person with a physical one. He had called out to what looked like thin air, 'Hey, Bob', before realizing that he had been mistaken and that the physical 'Bob' he was after was actually on the other side of the room. I had heard numerous other stories like that. On more than one occasion, I directly experienced him reading my mind and can only imagine what it was like for him to be in a room full of people, hearing the thoughts of all the physical people as well as seeing their extraphysical companions and hearing their thoughts, too! I often wondered what he was seeing when he looked at the space around my head, but I was too shy to ask.

Waldo did give large workshops. In Brazil he is a famous personality with regular media appearances and a national profile. Before adopting the scientific approach to consciousness with the development of conscientiology in the 1980s, he had been a significant figure in the Brazilian Spiritualist Church and had authored many channeled books, including some jointly with another famous Brazilian medium, Chico Xavier. While his move away from Spiritualism was highly controversial for some, his contribution in developing conscientiology was a significant evolutionary step from a much broader perspective. Consequently, it attracted a new generation of people who wanted to explore the reality of consciousness without relying on religious dogma or preconceived ideas. Because of this new approach and because of who he was, some of Waldo's courses were attended by several hundred people.

Courses I recall taking with him included Sex and Conscientiology, Cosmogramme, and Developing Energetic Sensitivity. But for me, the most impactful course I took was a three-day residential workshop called Extension in Conscientiology and Projectiology 2. It is the final stage of the core conscientiology curriculum, and it has a strong focus on energetic healing. As Waldo explains, it provides an energetic boost that allows the creation of new synapses, that is, new cerebral connections, which in turn assists us in changing our way of thinking and feeling.

One of the key components of this course was an intense energetic field, of which Waldo was the energetic epicenter. This means that he functioned as a channel for energy from the extra-physical dimension. The emphasis in this workshop was not on the transmission of verbal information but on producing an energetic realignment. Waldo would be seated in a large armchair at the head of the hall and enter into a trance state. This means that he was no longer in his body but was projected outside of it. An extraphysical team would then use his body as the centerpiece for generating the intense energetic field in the room. Participants had to do nothing more than lie on mats and relax. No technique, no trying to do anything, yet things would start happening to people. I don't know what other people sensed, but I experienced many energetic phenomena: intense pressures around different chakras, energies flowing out of my hands and feet, feelings of being disassociated from my body, and a complete distortion of time. The session would go on for a good two or three hours, but to me it seemed to pass in the blink of an eye. At some point, there would be a tangible shift in the energetic field, and participants would be invited to sit up. At this stage, the consciousnesses working through Waldo would be available to answer questions.

The first time I attended this workshop, I had been in Brazil just long enough to leave me feeling deeply confused. When I arrived, I suffered from a condition I have since dubbed the evolutionary (or spiritual) superiority syndrome. I had enjoyed so many peak experiences and spiritual insights in the past two years that clearly, I thought, I had to be *special*. It is a symptom I have since observed in others who engage in spiritual practices of one type or another. The irony was that I was actually deeply insecure and anxious in many areas of my life. So while I pursued and experienced states of great expansion of consciousness and encounters with extraphysical conscious-nesses in this and other dimensions, I struggled with a lot of the basics in life: sex, food, human relations and many other aspects of daily living still saw me largely governed by unconscious or semi-conscious automatic patterns. The study of the evolution of consciousness on the terms of conscientiology covers all of these areas and challenges us to bring our awareness into every area where automatism rears its head. In my case, part of my uncon-sciousness stemmed from my blindness to my own immaturities, a fairly common condition.

My spiritual superiority complex was challenged as soon as I began to immerse myself in conscientiology, because I came to realize how little I really knew and how unconscious of multidi-mensionality I really was. Despite all the peak experiences I had enjoyed, when it came to applying energetic control in the big city, I struggled. The IIPC had also not proven to be the welcoming spiritual haven I had anticipated. I clashed with people. And they were all very 'normal', not at all 'spiritual'. Worst of all, I seemed to be normal too!

So when it was my turn to address the extraphysical helpers working through Waldo's body, I found myself asking a question that, looking back, seems very naive but came from a true and deep sense of confusion: 'What am I supposed to do?' I actually think I asked the question in slightly tentative Portuguese, but the answer came back in very emphatic English and with an energetic charge that hit me right at the core: 'You have an extraphysical task. You are receiving assistance all the time.' Fifteen years later, I am still not entirely clear as to what this answer meant, but I do know that during various existential crises that followed, I received deep reassurance from the suggestion that I was being assisted by extraphysical helpers at all times. This early advice certainly helped to sustain me during my time in Rio, and it helped me recognize on various occasions this subtle extraphysical assistance.

Teaching Conscientiology

The IIPC is run almost entirely by volunteers. While Waldo gave some special and advanced courses, a cohort of trained volunteer instructors taught the day-to-day curriculum of projectiology and conscientiology. It was my immediate ambition to become an instructor, so I immersed myself in the classes, which in the Ipanema office were held three times a day: mornings, afternoons and evenings. Ironically, my evolutionary superiority complex served me quite well on the path towards becoming a conscientiology instructor, since it gave me a cockiness I might have otherwise lacked. As it was, I moved towards the goal of giving conscientiology classes at great speed despite the language barrier and the fact that I was absolutely terrified of standing in front of a room full of people.

In my experience, a conscientiology classroom is not like any other classroom, at least not for the teacher. As soon as you start talking, an extraphysical helper attaches him- or herself to you and provides assistance throughout the session while other helpers maintain the energetic field of the space and assist the students, either energetically or by 'whispering' in their ears to help them get ideas at a deeper level. While I only ever had the most fleeting visual perceptions of all this, I perceived these processes in a number of other ways. For one thing, despite my anxiety in those early days, once I started talking I became very calm. I would also feel myself almost continuously exteriorizing energy, which I perceived as a current emanating from me, although it actually came from the non-physical dimension and simply passed through me to 'thicken up' the energies, making them more useful for providing assistance to the physical and extraphysical people in the classroom. Ideas would start to flow and words would come out of my mouth that helped me to understand the concepts at a deeper level than I had before 'I' explained them to the students.

Teaching conscientiology is a great way to accelerate one's own evolution or personal growth, in part, because it helps us to understand concepts at a deeper level and confront any fears or inhibitions we may have about speaking about them in public. For me, it also provided a very direct way to confront old energetic ties like the one I broke when I had my 'death' experience in the Buddhist meditation session. In fact, one of the topics discussed in conscientiology classes is the relationship between physical and extraphysical people, in particular our relationships with *intruders* and *helpers*.

Intruders are a very important topic, because they impact all of us. But it is also a very large topic, and I will only briefly touch on it here. I have already provided some significant instances of interdimensional intrusion. The consciousness coupled with me from a past life and the disturbing voices in my head were both such cases. It was through the study of conscientiology that I really came to understand the virtually universal dynamic of intrusion. Intruders are sick consciousnesses, both extraphysical and intraphysical, who negatively influence people through their energies. You don't have to imagine anything fanciful to get the idea. They are not demons with horns and tails. If you have ever experienced being bullied, harassed, or manipulated through peer pressure or a misuse of power by another person; or if you have felt drained by someone who was stuck in blame and self-pity and tried to draw you into it; or if you have had a random stranger abuse or swear at you, then you have experienced intrusion. Intra- and extraphysical intruders are very much the same. At the extreme end they are complete psychopaths, deliberately seeking to harm others, but for the most part they are just self-absorbed and not very ethically attuned. They may have no sense of the negative energies they are emitting into the environment or of the fact that by attaching themselves to us they are making us feel unwell physically, emotionally or mentally. Intrusion by extraphysical consciousnesses is ubiquitous and comes into play in many cases of mental disturbance, physical ailments, addictions, accidents and any situation where intraphysical consciousnesses are cruel, violent and inhumane towards each other.

Sometimes when people first become aware of intrusion, there is a tendency to blame anything that does not work out well and all of humanity's cruelties on intruders. By taking that attitude, however, one positions oneself as a victim. It is important to emphasize here that we are not the passive victims of intrusion. For intrusion to take place, there needs to be an opening, energetic, emotional or mental. My acts of violence in past lives opened me up to intrusion in this one, but less dramatically, any unethical thought or action on our part can open the door. This is then exploited, consciously or unconsciously, by the intruders. In other words, intrusion involves a complex interplay between the intruder and the person suffering the intrusion, often with roots in our multiexistential history.

My own inner life while in Brazil provides a good example of this interplay. My notes from that time bear witness to my frequent mental and emotional turmoil when I first arrived in the country. Nothing out of the ordinary. Just commonplace insecurities, feelings of worthlessness and general self-image problems as well as a good dose of anxiety about daily survival issues. For example, I found a number of references in my journal to my fear that I would lose my job and end up on the street, despite the abundant evidence of both physical and extraphysical assistance around me that would never have allowed that to happen. I know that these kinds of anxieties and insecurities are very common, yet at the same time, I know that their cause in my own case was the result of my personal multiexistential trajectory. My close, long-term multidimensional companion, the woman from whom I was finally separated during the meditation on death, could not have been so intimately attached to me if our energies had not been compatible. In quite a number of my retrocognitions, I observed former selves who were emotionally imbalanced: angry, repressed, bitter and confused. These emotions correspond to the frequencies of dense extraphysical dimensions, and I am fairly confident that I have spent repeated intermissive periods in dimensions that are not very pleasant, places called 'hell realms' by Buddhists, or 'baratrospheric dimensions' in conscientiology. When we spend time in such dimensions, it leaves scars on our psychosoma, our emotional body. We are also likely to maintain energetic connections, both to those dimensions and to our fellow residents, after our next resoma. Until we transform our patterns of thought and emotion, or what conscientiology calls our 'thosenes' (short for 'THOught-SENtiment-Energy', explained in detail in Chapter 15), those scars remain unhealed and influential, and the energetic connections alive and operative. Consequently, we will be subject to seemingly inexplicable mental and emotional turmoil and open to intrusion by disturbed consciousnesses from those pathological dimensions during our physical waking state. We may also be returning to those dimensions during the night in instinctive unconscious projections that leave us feeling drained and irritated.

On the other hand, experiencing these kinds of dimensions is significant from an evolutionary perspective. Just as a counselor is better able to offer meaningful advice to a client whose state of consciousness he or she knows first hand, so our capacity for multidimensional assistance grows through first-hand experience of the depths into which an individual's consciousness can fall. Paradoxically, it is through delving into the abyss of self-centered suffering that we become able to soar to the heights of compassionate assistance to all other consciousnesses. To be able to draw on these experiences for assistance, we eventually need to transform our intimate state of being so that we are no longer the victims of our past. This may take more than one lifetime, but once we become aware that this is the process we are engaged in, it will occur.

Freeing ourselves from intrusion does not require us to fight external enemies, but it does require us to deal with our own internal processes and our energetic condition. In that sense, intruders are actually great teachers, because they will show us where our weaknesses and unresolved issues lie. The more stable we become energetically, emotionally and mentally, the less we are penetrable or susceptible to intrusion.

The first time I ever discussed this topic in class, the atmosphere in the classroom was instantly transformed. It seemed as if the walls were contracting, and I experienced brief red flashes before my eyes, felt a sense of pressure on my chest and struggled for air in order to keep talking. It only lasted a few seconds, half a minute at most, but it was very oppressive. I was not the only one who perceived this, either. The experienced instructor who was mentoring me at that stage of my training commented afterwards on the intensity of the energy during that part of the class. This was not the typical classroom experience for this topic, and it reflected the fact that I had come into this present lifetime with some very strong links to intrusive consciousnesses, and not just the one who was so closely coupled to me. Dealing with this head-on by discussing the topic in a conscientiology classroom was in itself an important step in transforming my relationship to those consciousnesses.

Fortunately, that topic was immediately followed by a discussion about helpers, those conscious individuals who dedicate much of their extraphysical time and energy assisting us to move through the challenges of physical life. Unlike intruders, helpers do not interfere with us against our will, even if it would sometimes be to our benefit. They are entirely ethical in their approach, and they respect our free will completely. They also have considerable insight into who we really are across lifetimes and beyond this current physical manifestation, and they know why we are here in this particular existence. Essentially, their desire is for us to achieve our full potential on our own steam so as to maximize the evolutionary benefits of the experience. People like Isaac and the other consciousnesses around Leia were all helpers. Helpers are fun, and as soon as I started talking about them, the energy in the room completely shifted. It became light and positive, and the sense of repression was replaced by a sense of joy, freedom and unconditional love.

Life in Rio de Janeiro

Much as I may have enjoyed my time in the conscientiology classroom, life in Rio de Janeiro was not so much fun. I longed for the tranquility of the English countryside. I still hoped I might move to Iguassu Falls, but it quickly became clear that I would not be getting out of the city any time soon. As far as conscientiology was concerned, the action was still in Rio de Janeiro. Today the campus in Iguassu Falls is the hub of conscientiology in Brazil. But in the late 1990s, that site was still in its early days of construction, and most of the activities that did occur there relied on the presence of Waldo and other instructors visiting from Rio.

So I settled into life in the big city. I had found a job teaching English and German, which provided me with enough money for my day-to-day living. I experienced extraphysical assistance not only in the way I found the job at a language school minutes away from the IIPC office in Ipanema, but also in the way it was made clear to me that I could relax once I had done so. I say 'made clear', because due to my habitual patterns of anxiety around survival, I initially felt compelled to keep seeking other jobs despite being offered the one at this perfect location very early into my hunt. After all, my responsible but anxious mind reasoned, the hours were casual and I could not be assured of enough work from this one place to cover my cost of living. So I kept contacting other schools and even contemplated taking on a job on the other side of the city, which would have seriously interfered with my conscientiology studies and volunteering at the IIPC. In taking this approach, I was acting from a particular psychological disposition that considered it necessary to work really hard to make sure that everything worked out, despite the reassuring voice that was telling me that things had already worked out and that I just needed to give my job in Ipanema a bit of time to develop. I finally accepted this voice when one day, as I was walking along a footpath, I looked down to find a business card from the language school in Ipanema. It took that tangible a message for me to allow myself to relax and trust.

Life in Rio was intense. Catching public transport frequently involved literally jumping onto the street to make sure the bus stopped. This was followed by a tight squeeze among commuters who were all thrown about as one bus raced another, with the drivers shouting out to each other in a language I was told even the locals could not understand. Poverty was ubiquitous. Slums hugged most of the hills that define the city, families actually lived in cardboard boxes, street kids roamed about, and drivers kept their doors locked for fear of assault as their vehicles stood still in the regular gridlock. Stories of people being shot so that someone could steal their pushbike or camera were all too common. At night, the bus would often skip certain stops for fear of a whole scale hijacking.

I lived in the suburb of Tijuca, at the bottom of a hill. At the top of the hill was a slum (*favela*), and on a number of occasions during my stay, the military police would assemble on our street before moving up the hill. Usually this would be followed by extended gunfire, including at times from what sounded like heavy weapons. The thought of stray bullets did cross my mind on more than one occasion. My closest personal brush with crime, however, happened on the bus. One evening, two fellows with clearly disturbed energies got on. One pushed into the seat next to mine and, with one hand under his shirt, either pointed or pretended to point a weapon at me. He was just starting to talk to me, no doubt with the intention of demanding my money or some other valuable, when his partner told him to leave me alone. They then hassled someone else instead, forcing the person to take off his sneakers before telling the driver to stop and getting off. For me, the illogical way in which they left me alone was an instance of extraphysical assistance.

Despite all this, my direct experience of the city was largely of friendly people who would engage in conversation with you on the street or in a shop. When Princess Diana died, a shop assistant expressed her most heartfelt consolation for the loss of 'my princess'. Seated passengers on buses would always volunteer to hold the bags of standing passengers, and I frequently saw these offers accepted and never any instance of theft. Rio is many things. It has a beautiful natural backdrop. It has warm, colorful and friendly people. It has wealth and a regular middle-class lifestyle, and it has abject poverty, crime and violence. Many people are also deeply religious. When a bus goes past a church, many of the passengers will make the sign of the cross, and it is very common to find offerings to extraphysical consciousnesses on the side of the street, placed there by practitioners of Umbanda, Candomblé or similar Afro-indigenous religions. All these factors together made for a very intense energetic and multidimensional environment, the extent of which became especially apparent to me only after my return from Brazil, when London suddenly seemed like a relaxing haven of calm and order!

There were many times when I wished to run away and return to my idyllic English countryside with its rolling hills, forests and empty beaches. But on those occasions, when I thought I could not stand it any longer, I would feel the gentle energetic presence of an extraphysical consciousness, or my attention would be directed to the one tree in the midst of the concrete jungle, and my energetic exchange with this tree would provide me with a boost. Rio also has stunning beaches, usually crowded and not always considered safe, but visiting them regularly helped me recharge my energetic battery.

Although I cannot say I enjoyed my stay in Rio, in hindsight it provided me with an excellent training ground and helped me develop much greater energetic self-reliance. My conscientiology studies and activities with the IIPC helped too, because they continuously kept me aware of the importance of working with energies and especially of applying a technique called the 'closed circulation of energies'. This is a very effective energetic self-defense technique. It enabled me to become increasingly able to sustain myself in very dense energetic environments, and even if I felt myself becoming unbalanced, once I started working with energy for a while, I would be able to sort myself out again.

Iguassu Falls

I did make it to Iguassu Falls once. I traveled to the nascent campus in December 1997 to attend a workshop given by Waldo called Developing Energetic Sensitivity, and I have to admit that

I fervently hoped I could find a way of staying there and getting out of Rio. At the time, the campus consisted of an events hall and a recently completed accommodation block that was inaugurated on the occasion of the workshop. There were two laboratories, the Three-Hour Waking Physical Immobility Laboratory and the Projectarium, which was also inaugurated during my stay.

Laboratories are an important part of conscientiology research. They are not like the labs of conventional science, which are equipped with high-tech devices to measure external units. Rather, they are spaces for self-research, and they are equipped with everything needed for optimal research conditions of this type: good climate control, sound insulation, pen and paper and comfortable beds or chairs, depending on the purpose of the lab. The spaces also have specific extraphysical infrastructures set up by extraphysical helpers to assist with the particular experiments for which each lab is designed. But the researchers themselves are the main piece of equipment. In conscientiology, the researcher is both the object of study *and* the subject doing the studying. In the Three-Hour Waking Physical Immobility Lab, for example, researchers make themselves comfortable in a reclining armchair and spend three hours staring at a blank white wall without moving any part of their bodies. Blinking and swallowing are also to be avoided, if possible. When you do this, you may start to develop a new relationship with your body. You may also experience energies in a new way, and you may have out-of-body experiences, although that is not the primary purpose of that lab. Since that time, many different labs have been developed at the campus, but in 1997, things were still just beginning.

There was a small team of volunteers living at Iguassu Falls who were basically in charge of developing the campus. I wanted to be a part of this. Surely that was why I had projected here when I was still living in England. I started to get excited. Yes, I would relocate and contribute to the construction of the campus! Not long after I made this mental decision, Waldo came towards me and without any preamble declared, 'It is not your time to stay here.' His words annoyed me. Why not? But I knew he was right. At least for now, my place was elsewhere.

I should perhaps clarify that I did not consider Waldo to be telling me this in the sense of giving me an order. Instead, I considered him to be conveying information from a perspective that enabled him to see the bigger picture. The information resonated with me. A part of me knew that I had other things to do, even if I was not very clear at that stage as to what they were. I could have stayed, of course. No one would have stopped me. But it would have just been stubborn of me, and I don't think I would have been happy for very long because those other things would have started niggling at me. So I returned to the big smoke of Rio for a little while longer.

The Green Crystal

You will recall the crystals, possibly extraphysical, that according to Leia are found at various locations around the planet. Earlier I described a projection I had while still in England, where I identified a green crystal below the waterfalls at Iguassu Falls. While I have not generally emphasized this point, there were many times when I questioned and requestioned the experiences I was having, including both the subtle perceptions of extra-physical consciousnesses and energies I encountered during my daily life, as well as my various projective experiences. Even after so many projections and different multidimensional perceptions, there remained a doubtful, questioning part of my mind that wondered whether I might be falsely interpreting something as a 'real' experience when it was actually some sort of psychological creation or sensory delusion. In the case of the crystals, I had seen them while I was projected, and in the past I had deliberately tuned into the white crystal and noticed tangible changes in my energetic body as a result. But despite all this, there remained a doubt in my mind as to their reality, and I wondered whether perhaps I had only perceived them on the basis of Leia's suggestion that they existed.

So during a group excursion to the waterfalls after which Iguassu Falls is named, I decided to tune into the supposed green crystal. The impact was undeniable but difficult to describe. Not only did I feel that I was a channel for an intense energy that moved through me and altered my energetic body; I also visually perceived a green hue starting to emanate from me. Waldo Vieira was on the excursion, and in hindsight I regret not asking him whether he could see any of this energy. That information could have provided me with more objective corroboration of this very curious phenomenon. Nonetheless, for me, personally, the evidence was undeniable and removed any doubts I might have had. I now fully accept the crystals as being part of the energetic system of planet Earth.

I would like to make just one final note on these crystals. On one occasion, I sought to project to the green crystal in an attempt to understand it better. In this projection, I entered a large room, like a vast cave, in which I found a variety of 'animals', including a giant spider. Even though these conscious-nesses manifested in animal bodies, they were not animal consciousnesses in the sense that they seemed well beyond that stage of evolution. I do not recall any communication as such, but the energies of these beings felt ancient, and my impression was that I was being allowed to visit. It was not something I could have done without their permission. Like the black panther, they seemed to be guardians or caretakers of the crystal. I had the sense that they looked after the energetic pathways of this planet and that they were related to the processes of nature. The totemic traditions of the world's indigenous peoples, in which the spirits of animals are revered, often associate such animal spirits with specific areas of land and attribute to them particular powers and significance. This experience has made me wonder whether some of these traditions are inspired by and relate to these ancient consciousnesses in animal guise.

Chapter 15

Controlling Energy and Helping Others

One of the things that helped me in Rio de Janeiro was doing lots of energy work. 'Energy work' here refers to a simple set of exercises any person can do with their energetic body, or energosoma. The energosoma covers the physical body like a sheath and penetrates every cell. It is a part of us and is controllable by our will. In Brazil I learned three basic techniques that can have a profoundly beneficial effect on our overall stability, well-being and psychic development if applied on a regular basis. All of these techniques are applied simply by focusing our intention on the desired movement of energy:

1. *The closed circulation of energies.* In this technique we move energy from the head to the feet and back up again, at ever increasing speed and intensity. The aim is to eventually reach a state where the entire energetic body is vibrating as one. This is called the vibrational state.

2. *Exteriorization of energy.* As the name suggests, in this technique we send out energy in all directions from the energetic body. This technique is useful when we want to cleanse our own energetic body and the surrounding space, or assist others.

3. *Absorption of energy.* In this technique, we draw energy in from the environment in order to vitalize ourselves. This technique should only be applied in spaces where the energies are positive, for example, at sites rich in natural energy.

The closed circulation of energies kept me functioning in Rio de Janeiro. I would do it on the bus or while walking, before and after language classes, and when I got home. Occasionally, I would go to the beach to connect with the ocean and absorb energies from there, always being cautious not to draw in energies from the crowds that frequent Rio's beaches.

Developing Our Energetic Muscle

The term 'energy' gets used quite a lot these days, and sometimes it can seem esoteric or vague, but it is really something very tangible. We can feel it and manipulate it simply through the force of our intention. When I talk about moving energy up and down, sending it out or drawing it in, I am talking about doing so simply by mentally expressing our intention and focusing our will. The energy of our energosoma is a part of us, just like our arms or hands. And just as we do not need to visualize anything to open and close our hand, so we do not need to visualize ourselves moving energy. We just intend to do it. Like any new skill, when we first start we might find it difficult to perceive energy. We might find that it does not readily obey our commands, or we may notice blocks in the energy body. But with persistent practice, everybody can feel energy and make it flow. It is part of our physiology or, perhaps better, our *paraphysiology*.

I encourage you to try the following exercise.

Sit comfortably, with a straight back and your arms and legs uncrossed. Spend a few moments relaxing your body, starting with your feet and then moving up to your calves, thighs, abdomen, chest, shoulders, back, neck and face, relaxing each body part in turn.

Next, extend your awareness beyond the limits of your skin to see whether you get any sense of your energetic body. Allow a few moments for this, but whether you perceive anything or not is irrelevant at this point. Just mentally express the intention for your energy to gather around the top of your head. Allow a few minutes for this, simply repeating in your mind the intention for the energy to accumulate around the crown of your head.

Once you feel you have allowed enough time for the energy to accumulate, start moving it downwards by giving it the mental instruction to do so. If you can perceive an accumulation, follow it down with your awareness until you reach your feet. Then bring it back up to your head and continue this up-and-down movement for several minutes.

If you do not feel any energy, just focus your intention on moving the energy up and down anyway while remaining mindful of your body. Gradually intend the energy flow to speed up and increase in intensity, always maintaining your awareness of any sensations in and around your body.

Ultimately you will want to speed up the flow to such an extent that it stops being a flow and your entire energetic body vibrates as one. That is the vibrational state. If you reach this state, hold it for a few minutes.

It may take time to achieve this state. Some find it easier than others, depending on personal conditions and multiexistential (past-life) experiences with energy. But whatever your position right now, if you persist, you will definitely be able to move energy and achieve the vibrational state. Along the way, you may notice all kinds of unusual sensations as you continue your intention of moving energy. These may include changes in body temperature, pulsating and tingling sensations, activation of certain chakras, loss of body awareness and a sense of expansion, and so on. These symptoms can arise whether you believe in energy or not, simply from focusing your intention on moving it.

Once you are able to install the vibrational state, you will find it invigorating and rejuvenating. Over time it will help you to unblock your energetic body, and if you build it into your daily life, it can be an invaluable prophylactic against intrusive energetic influences, which unfortunately are all around us. Once you get the hang of this energetic movement, it is something you can do in any life situation: while maintaining a conversation, standing in line or reading a book. The same applies to the other two movements of absorption and exteriorization, and the general approach is the same. Energy will follow your intention. If you want it to flow from you it will, and if you want to absorb it, you will draw it in. In most cases, you will want to ensure that the energy you absorb is from a source of pure, raw natural energy. In conscientiology such energy is called **immanent energy** and we can find it at oceans, wilderness areas and other sites not impacted by what is called **consciential energy**, that is, energy molded through the thoughts and emotions of various consciousnesses.

Assisting with Energy

In addition to being important to our own well-being, a healthy energosoma is also the primary means by which we can assist the people around us. If our own energies are healthy and flowing freely, we can use them to balance the energies of spaces and people, both physical and extraphysical. This understanding is shared by many of the experiential spiritual traditions. In Mahayana Buddhism, for example, people meditate not only to calm their minds or experience altered states of consciousness, but because they believe that one person's meditation can positively impact others. In that tradition, meditations are regularly dedicated to 'all sentient beings'. I felt intuitively drawn to this approach when I was going through my Buddhist period, but it was only once I studied conscientiology that I understood the technical aspects of this type of assistance.

There are a number of levels to energetic assistance. The first is the small contribution made by the frequency of our personal mental energies to the ocean of energy created by our collective mental and emotional processes. Conscientiology has coined the term *thosene* to describe the manner in which our energies are generated. The word 'thosene' is a compound made up of the following elements: THOught/SENtiment/Energy. The term succinctly captures the fact that we are always producing these three elements in unison. Every thought is accompanied by an emotion or sentiment and vice versa, even if the ratio of the two varies at different times. For example, when we look into the eyes of a lover or when we support our favorite sports team during a cliff-hanger match, sentiments will outweigh thoughts. But when we write an essay or play chess, thought will outweigh emotion. Whatever the ratio of the two, they always produce energy. The three are inseparable. That is why it is more accurate to speak of *thosene-ing* rather than thinking or feeling.

Naturally, over the period of a day, we will experience all kinds of different thosenes. We may feel worried or stressed at one point and relaxed and positive at another. We might be clear-minded or confused, focused or distracted, and so on. But overall, each of us has a basic pattern, an average level of vibration based on our overall patterns of thinking and feeling. This is what is called our personal *holothosene*. 'Holo-' here means 'whole set', so the holothosene is the set of our thosenes as a whole. Another way of thinking about this is that our holothosene is our fundamental vibrational frequency, which is caused by our default pattern of thinking and feeling. Consider the following states of mind many of us go through every day: anxiety, fearfulness, resentment, regret, repression, boredom, anger, dishonesty towards ourselves and others, excessive focus on our lack or desire in such areas as sex, money and love. If we accept that these are all common human experiences, it is easy to see that for many of us our holothosenes are dominated by emotions that relate largely to a perspective of ourselves limited to this current physical life. A holothosene generated from a strong sense of the multi-lifetime, multidimensional perspective of consciousness would look quite different.

All of us generate our own holothosene bubbles, and in doing so we impact the world around us, because energy extends beyond the individual. It is not confined to the limits of our physical bodies. Many people have had the experience of reacting to another's energies. We might say that a given person 'feels creepy', or we might notice ourselves feeling buoyant after spending time with one person yet feel drained by another. We might think we have been uplifted by one person's great ideas or exhausted by another who talks too much, but what we are really reacting to are the individual holothosenes of the different people. People's holothosenes do not just impact on those they meet; they also impact on the environment in which they move. Our homes are inevitably reflections of our holothosenes. I am not here referring to the decorations or the state of tidiness. These things can sometimes be an indication, but they can also be deceiving. The real impact is found in the energies, the overall vibration of the place.

If you bring a group of people together for an extended period of time, say at a workplace or in a town, their individual holothosenes will combine to create a collective holothosene. Within the group, there may be people with different emphases: the more emotional holothosene versus the more intellectual one, the more self-centered one versus the more empathetic one; but ultimately there will be an overall pattern. This is true of your local street, your suburb and your city. It applies wherever groups of people come together. So, the most fundamental type of assistance any of us can provide is to alter our own holothosene so that its contribution to the larger collective holothosene raises rather than depresses the energetic field.

The most immediate way to achieve this is to focus ourselves predominantly in the mentalsoma, the body of consciousness that vibrates at the highest frequency range. The perspective of the mentalsoma is the most detached, compassionate and serene, devoid of the emotions of the psychosoma and free from any egocentric survival drives arising from the body. From this perspective, we are aware of our true reality as ancient and immortal consciousnesses on a journey with millions of evolutionary colleagues. Most of us will only be able to tap into this perspective intermittently, during moments of reflection or contemplation. But whenever we do, we are contributing positive, expansive energies to those around us. While this contribution may seem subtle and infinitesimal, the effect of even one person focusing his or her awareness at that level of consciousness will introduce energies into the collective holothosene that will help others who are seeking greater lucidity within this dense physical dimension. This kind of assistance is essentially impersonal in that it is not directed towards one particular individual, and it usually goes unnoticed. But it is not to be underestimated.

A second form of energetic assistance is more personal and in some ways more direct. It involves using the energies of our own energetic body to balance and provide direct assistance to the energetic bodies of others, both intra- and extraphysical. I first had the experience of providing assistance to extraphysical consciousnesses when applying the B-ing meditation I had learned at Shanti Loka. For two or three years after learning it, I would practice it every day, usually in the mornings. I would either sit in a chair or lie on my bed and go through my different body parts, and then I would hold my awareness of the whole body for a long time before 'letting go'. In practicing this technique, I experienced many strange sensations, some of which I already described earlier. But there is one particular sensation I have not yet described in detail. This was the feeling of 'being' another person. It could include unfamiliar thoughts running through my head, feelings that just did not seem like mine, and sometimes whole scenarios involving relationships with other people and particular life events, none of which had any meaning for me.

One of the most intense of these experiences happened while I was traveling in western Romania. I was applying the meditation on my bed in a tiny mountain village when the most intense feeling came over me. I could tell that the person I was sensing was a young man. There was a lot of fear and guilt, and I could tell that he (although it felt more like 'me' at the time) had been beaten to death by a group of men because he had raped a young girl. The words 'baci eu' were etched into my mind. A couple of days later, I had the opportunity to check a dictionary and discovered that 'baci eu' meant 'shepherd I', both a clue as to the identity of the young man and a comforting indication to my ever questioning mind that the experience was something real. Even though I did not fully understand the process at that point, it was very clear to me on this occasion that I had in some way assisted a 'dead' man in releasing old energies.

Waldo Vieira has developed both a description and a technical approach relating to this kind of assistance. He refers to the energetic exchange that happens in such instances as a process of sympathetic assimilation and deassimilation of energies that allows one consciousness to take on and transmute the thosenic blockages or baggage of another. In this case, this consciousness had been holding on to his energetic body after his violent and fearful death. In practical terms, maintaining his energetic body after his physical body had been deactivated would have meant that he was in a state of highly restricted lucidity, essentially caught in the unpleasant sensations of his last life. The kind of consciousnesses people commonly perceive as 'ghosts' or the ones depicted in numerous TV shows as not having entirely 'passed over' are examples of people who are still holding on to the dense energetic body from their last physical lifetime. My contribution in Romania was to donate the dense semi-physical energy of my energetic body, which the extraphysical helpers used to liberate this consciousness from his now redundant energosoma, thereby allowing him to move on.

For me, and no doubt for many others who practice meditation or energy techniques, this assistance happened spontaneously. I had not deliberately set out to achieve this result, nor did I even understand the process at the time. Conscientiology, however, has developed a technical process of assistance that draws on this dynamic. It is called the Personal Energetic Task, or Penta for short, and it involves a daily commitment to exteriorize energies for 50 minutes for the benefit of other consciousnesses, both intraphysical and extraphysical ones. Just as with my experience in Romania, the energetic exteriorization that occurs during Penta is not driven solely by the intention of the intraphysical practitioner. Instead, the physical person becomes part of a team of extraphysical helpers who specialize in the kind of assistance delivered through Penta, and who guide and manage the process. It is through a practice like Penta that we establish the extraphysical office I mentioned when I described some of the assistance I believe Leia was doing. Over time, our regular energetic exteriorizations will allow the helpers to create such an 'office' where they can attend to ill extraphysical and projected intraphysical consciousnesses beyond the brief periods of the actual Penta sessions themselves. The intraphysical consciousness functions primarily as a channel or conductor for the subtle energies of extraphysical specialists. The dense energies carried by the physical human's energosoma act as a conduit for the extraphysical helpers so that it can provide assistance to other intra- and extraphysical consciousnesses with dense energies.

The process described above, of helping people to shed the dense energies of the energosoma after they have gone through the death of the physical body, is one of the direct applications of Penta. As I have already explained, people often instinctively hold on to these energies, largely for psychological reasons such as physical attachments or fear and ignorance about life beyond matter. In the extraphysical dimension, the energetic body is very dense and carries many of the thosenic patterns of the past life. This means that if people carry them around after deactivating their soma, they will continue to feel largely like they did while still in the physical body. In a healthy death, we will shed those energies not long after we shed the physical body and by doing so free ourselves from the restrictions of physical life. We will not be transformed into somebody completely different, but we will enjoy mental and emotional freedom beyond our common human experience, and we will be able to gain greater awareness of our true nature as a multidimensional consciousness. If we hold on to the energies, on the other hand, they will keep us emotionally and mentally stuck in the most intense experiences of our past lives. The shepherd in Romania had been in that situation. The reason I felt his emotions and perceived his memories so directly was because my energies were used to help strip him of his own so that he could move on.

Another application of Penta is to facilitate the process of deintrusion. Deintrusion refers to the act whereby one consciousness or a group of consciousnesses assists in the removal of intrusive consciousnesses from the sufferer of the intrusion. The removal of my long-term companion was an act of deintrusion. In that case it was a complicated situation involving the input of a number of helpers, including Pak Suyono and Leia. Other cases of intrusion may be less chronic and therefore resolvable through a single energetic intervention. Sometimes the presence of a person with high-level energies can lead to temporary deintrusion, because the intrusive consciousnesses can't stand being within the energetic space that this consciousness (a 'consciential epicenter') creates. But more permanent deintrusion usually requires a thosenic shift on the part of both the sufferer and the perpetrator of the intrusion. The extraphysical office can provide a space where helpers are able to communicate with both individuals involved in the dynamic and provide a form of paracounseling to help them adjust their thosenic postures and thereby release each other from their energetic entanglement.

One key purpose of life is for consciousnesses to help each

other. There are many ways in which this can happen. Some forms of assistance focus on physical interventions such as primary health care or providing food and shelter. Others focus on emotional support to help people feel better. Still others provide assistance through ideas by teaching or providing added mental clarity in some other way. Parents who raise their children in a loving and supportive home are assisting those consciousnesses, as are people who give of their time to a humanitarian cause, be it supporting the disadvantaged, working for human rights, feeding the hungry, creating better living conditions, helping people to deal with the aftermath of trauma, and so on.

All such activities are valuable in principle, but their real value is often determined by the energies of the people doing the assistance. If the person providing aid in the form of food is bitter and resentful, or if the teacher who has come to provide education to a disadvantaged community is self-righteous and arrogant, these traits will be reflected in the individual's holothosene, and they will have a very real impact on the people they are supposedly 'assisting'. On the other hand, those with balanced emotions, a clear mind and a healthy energetic body will be providing assistance wherever they go, if in no other way than by improving any energetic environment they enter.

When we commit ourselves to a practice like Penta, we are signing up as a small but important intraphysical piece in a large multidimensional system of selfless service. This service is ultimately about helping others. We do not enter it for personal gain or even to help our nearest and dearest. It is one hour a day we spend allowing our energies to be used to assist unknown and, to us, random strangers according to the priorities of the helpers. But as with any action that involves reaching out to others, we always benefit. In the case of a practice like Penta, we obtain the assistance of highly skilled extraphysical helpers, not only for the 50 minutes of the practice but continuously, 24 hours a day, seven days a week. And as we grow in our practice, so the extent of our energetic assistance will grow, gradually, from the brief dedicated sessions to a 24-hour service as the helpers naturally employ our energies to assist those around us in our daily lives. We will start to experience first hand the difference our energies can make in the environment and become more aware of the energetic impact of extraphysical intrusion. Gradually, we will grow into lucid energetic epicenters with a beneficial impact on whatever environment we enter, both in the physical and extraphysical dimensions. If we make this a priority, becoming such an assistential epicenter is achievable in this very lifetime.

Chapter 16

Helpers

I have already discussed helpers, mainly in the context of their role in facilitating projections of consciousness and working with us to give assistance. Because our relationship with helpers is a very important aspect of our evolutionary journey, I have dedicated a few pages to this topic here.

Just to be clear, the term 'helper' in this book refers to an extraphysical consciousness who provides assistance to us during our period as an intraphysical consciousness. Of course, sometimes physical people can also act in the capacity of helpers (Pak Suyono, Leia and Waldo are all in that category), but in this section, I am specifically focusing on the assistance given by extraphysical helpers. Such assistance can relate to our physical lives, our projections or the transition to our inevitable extraphysical life. Helpers are not angels, saints or divine beings. Most helpers who provide us with direct assistance are people of a similar evolutionary level as ourselves. The main difference between us is that they have the temporary benefit of not being confined by the limitations of the physical body at this point in time. It is entirely possible that we will return the favor during our next intermissive period while our current helpers experience the restrictions of a physical life.

Occasionally, we might encounter or receive assistance from more advanced helpers. This is most likely to occur if we ourselves are contributing to some more substantial process of assistance that involves these more advanced consciousnesses.

When I talk about a consciousness being 'more advanced', I am not suggesting that one consciousness is fundamentally better than another. We are all moving on the same evolutionary trajectory from a state of less consciousness and energetic control towards states of ever increasing consciousness and energetic control. So far, I have not encountered any answers as to why or how it all started, but I am certain that we are on this kind of journey. Along the way, there seem to be specific evolutionary conquests or stages that represent inevitable waypoints on our path towards multidimensional maturity. Among a number of those waypoints, conscientiology identifies three key stages.

The first of these is achieving a state of balance where we are totally and permanently free of intrusion. When a consciousness reaches this state, it is no longer impacted by energetic, emotional or mental intrusions, whether they are deliberate attacks or unconscious intrusions from either extra- or intraphysical consciousnesses. In order to realize what a significant achievement this is, it is worth pausing to consider all the intrusions we may have experienced over just the past few hours, manifesting for example as passing irritations, or feelings of stress, anxiety and frustration. Being totally and permanently intrusion-free means that we always maintain our energetic, emotional and mental equilibrium, regardless of any personal slights, misfortunes or challenging situations. People who have reached this stage are veritable pillars of harmonious energy, whatever environment or dimension they enter. Their very presence balances and harmonizes the thosenes of those around them, both physical and extraphysical. One of the challenges issued by Waldo is to strive to reach this stage in our current lifetime. It would be an evolutionary conquest that would accompany us from that point onwards and truly allow us to aim for the next stages. In other words, being totally and permanently intrusion-free is not the end of our journey: rather, it marks a beginning from which we can be much more deliberate and focused in planning our subsequent evolutionary lessons and undertakings.

The next stage identified in conscientiology is that of the evolutiologist. These consciousnesses have all the energetic presence of those who are totally and permanently intrusion-free and more! In addition to being energetic giants, they have also developed an incredible multidimensional perspective. Each evolutiologist is responsible for managing the evolution of millions of consciousnesses. This involves the coordination of mutually compatible life paths and of vast processes of assistance across dimensions. The members of any given evolutionary group (a group of consciousnesses currently moving through a particular evolutionary cycle together) are found both in the intraphysical and in various extraphysical dimensions, depending on their personal circumstances at any given moment. We will live many lives permanently and totally intrusion-free, assuming ever greater evolutionary and assistential responsibilities, before we become Evolutiologists.

The final evolutionary stage at which consciousnesses still manifest in this physical dimension is what Waldo Vieira has called the *Homo Sapiens Serenissimus* or just *Serenissimus* for short. This adaptation of the regular term *Homo Sapiens* reflects a key feature of these consciousnesses. They emanate utter serenity and peace wherever they are. A consciousness at this stage is in the process of completing its final intraphysical existences. It knows that the end is in sight and has mapped out its final activities, evolutionary tasks and karmic responsibilities in very precise detail. Waldo estimates that there are 50 to 60 of these personalities around planet Earth at present in both the physical and extraphysical dimensions. Those in the physical dimension are leading anonymous lives without any outward appearance of either spiritual or temporal power, yet their energies do a great deal to ensure that life on this planet continues and that the human follies so evident wherever one looks are checked to a certain degree so that we don't self-destruct. You may recall my earlier explanation of how our individual energetic contribution to the collective holothosene can make a positive difference. The energetic contribution of the *Homo Sapiens Serenissimus* ameliorates the holothosene of entire continents. I am assuming that the Boardroom as described by Leia is either made up of or at least includes these *Homo Sapiens Serenissimus*.

So how do helpers help? One of the core principles of multidimensional helpers is respect for the free will of those being helped. Helpers do not force, manipulate or coerce the intraphysical consciousness, even if it may seem to be in the latter's best interest. But they may try to provide some rather clear tips as to what might be a better choice in any given circumstance. Such tips can take the form of energetic signals, for example, a sudden shiver or energetic sensation. Sometimes they are conveyed telepathically through insights or hunches. And sometimes they even involve the manipulation of the physical environment, from changing the temperature of the shower as a gentle reminder of the helper's presence to actually tampering with the people around us. Once you realize how frequently we are all used as mediums by extraphysical consciousnesses, that is, once you realize how often physical people unconsciously channel the thoughts of extraphysical people, even if only for a few moments, you start listening to the people in your life as potential unconscious mouthpieces for your helpers (but also for your intruders!).

During my year in Brazil, I received extraphysical assistance on every level. There was the energetic assistance that would provide me with a lift when feeling tired or overwhelmed. I might be walking along and suddenly perceive a wave of energy flowing over me or spontaneously break out in a vibrational state. There were also instances when I was given more physical signs, such as noticing the business card of my employer on the pavement. And helpers facilitated numerous psychic events, including projections of consciousness and multidimensional perceptions.

For example, one Sunday my bus traveled past a large square. Families were walking, old men and women were sitting on benches chatting, children were playing. Suddenly I had a perception, like an inner knowing, that these same consciousnesses had shared a previous life in some city in southern France, where an almost identical scene had taken place in a square some 100 to 200 years ago. This was not something I had been thinking about. The idea just suddenly arose in my mind like a communication intended to teach me about our journeys across lifetimes within a large interconnected group of fellow travelers.

One really important role of helpers, however, is at first sight less glamorous than making our life circumstances work out or giving us great psychic insights. But it is perhaps the most significant. This is the assistance they provide us in overcoming our own psychological neuroses, immaturities and conditionings; in other words, helping us to change our thosenes. As already explained, changing our thosenes will gradually enable us to more permanently proof ourselves against intrusion. At times, I felt like I was being trained by an extraphysical coach whose main teaching tool was to induce certain psychological reactions by creating situations that functioned as perfect triggers. This might have involved the things people said to me, objects around me that suddenly jumped into my awareness, or sudden bursts of awareness about aspects of my own behavior or inner mental processes that had previously been hidden from me.

One especially pertinent example of this training occurred with respect to my psychological posture regarding my relationship with money. I had what could perhaps best be described as 'poverty consciousness'. I was consistently concerned about a lack of money, and I was regularly triggered to react with a feeling of being 'ripped off' when I felt that someone was charging too much for something I wanted. In England, my regular breakfast had consisted of a large bowl of muesli, but in Brazil I found that a very small bag of muesli cost more than my hourly teaching rate. Every time I saw the price of muesli, it triggered a mental monologue about the absurdity of this outrageous situation. Now it is true that I was not earning a lot of money, and the muesli was indeed more expensive than it had been in England. But my compulsive mental outbursts were a sign of deep-seated unresolved issues around my relationship with money that showed up in my view of people's intentions and my role as a victim, evidenced by such thoughts as, 'They are ripping me off.' I could probably find the sources of these mental attitudes in my current lifetime. My upbringing, for example, despite being generally middle class, had involved a certain sense of frugality. But I am quite certain that my issues had their source further back, before this physical body. The muesli brought out a more deeply rooted thosenic vulnerability, which in turn presented a great anchor point for mental intrusion by more conscious intruders who may have wanted to amplify my internal imbalance.

This thosene pattern manifested regularly when shopping. One day, I discovered some German black bread called Pumpernickel in a supermarket. Not only was it German, but it had actually been made in my hometown. I just had to have a loaf! As I looked at the price tag on the shelf, the numbers changed before my eyes. They 'shape-shifted' from the actual price to a figure at least twice as much. Despite the fact that I saw the shift happening right before my eyes, I still felt a sense of outrage welling up within me over the price. Then the figures shifted back again to the regular price. It was still not a cheap item, being a European import, but in comparison it now seemed reasonable! Suddenly, I understood the relativity of monetary value and the absurdity of my reactions. It was all just in my mind, not 'out there' in the world. It would be an exaggeration to say that this incident completely shifted my mental posture on this issue. That took a few more years. But it brought to my attention the relative nature of this perspective, that there was no solid 'truth' in my thoughts and that I could let go of this particular perspective if I so chose. It also reminded me of the remarkable ability extraphysical helpers possess for manipulating our perceptions of the intraphysical environment, and even the environment itself.

Working with helpers is a partnership. We are the less conscious member of the team, but that does not mean that we follow blindly or passively. As the old saying goes: helpers help those who help themselves. If, to the best of our ability, we move ahead with awareness and multidimensional attentiveness in the directions that call us, our helper or helpers will move ahead with us. The more we focus our efforts on assistance, the more we will be in harmony with our helpers, and we will increasingly be involved in projects managed by more evolved helpers. Gradually, we will assume our roles as mini-pieces in the massive process of assistance that is taking place across all dimensions on this planet. Most of us, most of the time, will only get a very slight sense of all the assistential works we become involved in, as this work is largely extraphysical and beyond most people's perceptions. But any glimpse we may get, during projections or through other psychic perceptions, of this vast, complex and compassionate process managed by the mega-helpers is deeply humbling, inspiring and incredibly enriching to our lives.

Chapter 17

Projections of Consciousness

One of the key research tools of conscientiology is the projection of consciousness. Leaving our physical bodies with awareness not only helps us to experience and learn about multidimensional life first hand, but over time it can also remove our fear of physical death. Once we truly come to know ourselves as beings who can live separately from the physical body, we can approach life from a very different perspective and set priorities that go beyond the trappings of physical survival. Of course, the relationship to the physical body is not transformed after only one or even a dozen projections. For most people, it requires many lucid experiences outside the physical body.

Although I experienced many projections over the two years prior to coming to Brazil, and although I also came to realize that I had experienced them already as a child without understanding what they were, once I met Waldo I quickly recognized how limited my own experiences in this area had really been. His books clearly spell out the level of control and awareness that is possible, which made me realize that I had never really felt in control of my projections. I was usually unable to leave my body at will. The experiences only happened spontaneously, and I seemed to have very little control over the degree of lucidity I could sustain when outside of the body.

The most striking example of this occurred some time prior to going to Brazil. I was in a lucid state as I gently glided out of my physical body to find a man sitting in a chair next to my bed. He was tall, clean-shaven with a bald head, and very strong looking. He had been focused on something else, but as soon as he noticed me rising up, he nodded in my direction and I lost consciousness completely. Interestingly, he had felt very much like a positive consciousness, a helper. But for some reason, this helper did not want me to be lucid.

In Brazil, I learned that there were good reasons why a helper might not want the projector to be conscious. Reducing the projector's level of awareness outside the body can be one way of looking after his or her well-being. For example, sometimes people might start to neglect their physical life duties (work, studies, family and so on) while pursuing peak experiences in other dimensions. In those cases, the pursuit of the 'spiritual life' through extraphysical experiences leads to an alienation from intraphysical life. I have seen this pattern in some of my friends and have observed aspects of it in myself as well. It is probably a natural part of the evolutionary journey to spend some periods more intensely focused on the subtle dimensions, especially when we first discover that aspect of life. But we are in this dimension for a reason, and it usually involves leading both a strong and productive intraphysical life *and* developing our awareness of multidimensionality. If we chronically neglect the former in favor of the latter, our helpers will be doing us a favor by shutting down our subtle perceptions for a while in order to force our attention back onto physical matters.

But there is another reason why a limited awareness might be in our own best interest. Being able to perceive some of the tasks for which projectors are at times used by helpers could be very disturbing. I have previously mentioned that the dense semi-physical energies carried by projectors in their energosomas allow them to play an important role as energetic conduits so that more subtle extraphysical consciousnesses can transmit therapeutic energies into dense dimensions. This process is similar to channeling, which is when an intraphysical consciousness temporarily allows his or her body to be used by an extraphysical consciousness to communicate with this dimension.

The same dynamic, whereby a consciousness in a denser

vehicle serves as a temporary channel for a subtler one, applies to the extraphysical dimensions. Just as most intraphysical people cannot see extraphysical consciousnesses, so disturbed 'dead' consciousnesses who have held on to their energetic bodies and still retain strong physical impulses cannot perceive subtle extraphysical consciousnesses. This is where projectors come in, in that they play the role of multidimensional mediums. As explained earlier, their dense energies, combined with their positive assistential thosenes, mean that they can manifest in denser dimensions while still being compatible with the helpers.

The dimensions where disturbed extraphysical consciousnesses live can be very distressing, the sites of frightening violence and cruelty worthy of any horror movie, a genre that is in fact an energetic channel for these kinds of dimensions. Many of my recollections from sleep, usually dreamlike and not of the same quality as a conscious projection, involved scenes of great violence and disturbed people. I am sure that at least some of those were the hazy memories of semi-lucid projections in which I played an assistential role under the guidance of lucid helpers. For example, projectors are sometimes used to conduct what in conscientiology is known as 'extraphysical rescues'. In such rescues, consciousnesses stuck in dense dimensions, but with a thosenic openness to moving to healthier environments, are assisted in that process by teams of helpers and projectors. A subtle indicator of having played such a role can be waking up with a sense of inner contentment or even mild euphoria that may seem quite incongruous with the memories from sleep. This emotion is the result of a productive night of service.

I must admit, despite the sense of being useful outside of the body, I was disappointed with my lack of progress. I had hoped the intensive study of projectiology, the specific study of the projection of consciousness, would allow me to take full control of the projective experience. But that was not to be. Even in Brazil, my projections continued as they had, seemingly at the whim of my helpers. My usual pattern, then as now, was to lie down with the intention of maintaining my awareness in the sleep state. I would essentially apply the Shanti Loka technique of being aware of my body as it fell asleep. Very commonly, I would then become aware of my psychosoma. I might also be aware of my body while it slept and occasionally even hear it snore. Sometimes my paralegs or para-arms would leave the body, and I would feel them floating up; or my whole psychosoma would be floating about except for my head, which would still be stuck inside my physical head. At other times, I would be briefly aware of shifting or floating out of the physical body in my psychosoma. Usually, I would lose consciousness at that point. I would then either recall very little from my extracorporeal experience, or find myself deeply embedded in dream imagery and my own thought creations. That meant that my thoughts were creating my reality while I was outside the body, thus cutting me off from the underlying reality of the extraphysical dimensions I was visiting.

This principle is not hard to understand. Most of us will be able to relate to a time when some mental preoccupation shut down our awareness of the world around us to the point that we couldn't recall why we came into the kitchen or how we got home from the office. Extraphysically, this process is amplified, because our thosenes actually create tangible thought-forms (morphothosenes) that can seem perfectly real to us, so it is easy to see how one can get caught in a world of one's own making.

A couple of times during this period, I experienced what is known as sleep paralysis or projective catalepsy, accompanied by extraphysical perceptions. On one occasion, I lay down midmorning after teaching an early morning English class. Following a range of energetic phenomena, I started hearing people walking around me. I could not see anything, nor could I move any part of my body, but I could hear heavy footsteps moving around me and people talking incomprehensibly. It was as if someone or something was checking me out. I knew that I could have broken the paralysis and woken myself up if I had wanted to. But even though the lack of control was somewhat disconcerting, I did not think that the people around me were dangerous, and I was curious to see whether I could enhance my extraphysical perceptions of them, but without success.

While a part of me was disappointed with my lack of progress with conscious projections, another part knew that the priority for my life was to integrate all my multidimensional perceptions, including those that occurred during the waking state and those that involved a departure from the physical body, with a fully functioning physical life. In England, I had been able to pursue my experiences of consciousness as a semi-recluse, spending hours in meditation every day. In Brazil, I had no such luxury. The environment was intense, I needed to work and commute, and I had joined a group of evolutionary colleagues who challenged me with demands for physical productivity. So for purely practical reasons, my priority was to live well in the physical dimension and not get lost in the extraphysical, something that had been tempting for me since my visit to Shanti Loka.

It is also true, though, that I struggled with an area that defines others who have written extensively about their projections of consciousness. Waldo Vieira, Robert Monroe, William Buhlmann, Jurgen Ziewe and numerous similar authors and researchers all have in common not only lucid projections but also excellent recall and the discipline of waking up and immediately recording their experiences. The following projective account from my journal of the time bears testament to the importance of such discipline:

Night from 15 April to 16 April 1998. A very lucid experience which I did not write down immediately and which now has become very hazy. A meeting organized by Leia concerning the upcoming awakening of somebody. This somebody would be the second half of a couple to awaken. Together, the energies of the two could cause some serious changes on the planet. It's for these changes, energetic changes, that we are preparing.

This excerpt is tantalizing: who is this couple and what is their intraphysical task? But it is basically of no analytical value because I omitted writing down the experience straight away when it was still fully within reach of my memory. In this case I had allowed another period of sleep to interfere with my recall of the experience. But it is also a fact that, unless we enjoy the evolutionary conquest of a particularly good memory, for most of us, projective experiences that are not pinned down straight away are lost very quickly upon waking, once our minds shift to dealing with the needs of the physical body.

It was never the intention of this book to recount a string of such experiences. There are many books with much more detailed accounts of this type than I would be able to furnish (you can find some of these at the end of this book). I would, however, like to relate just two of the more significant experiences from that year.

The first happened on my birthday in 1997. I had gone to sleep that night wishing for projections with full lucidity. The next thing I became aware of was of shooting into space as I was carried along by a consciousness who felt as old as time itself. I did not see him, but I felt his energies penetrating and carrying me along at great speed, and the mental image I received was of an ancient man with hardly any hair and wrinkly to the point where age becomes meaningless, but with incredibly powerful energy. I felt overwhelmed by the intensity of both the speed of the movement and the energies of this consciousness, and I found myself wanting to go back to my body. As if in response this happened momentarily, and as I shot back towards my physical vehicle I telepathically heard the ancient one laugh, with words to the effect of: 'You want to be lucid, but you can't handle this!' He was mocking me, but it actually felt like a birthday present and a sobering lesson regarding my own maturity. It was clear to me that if I wanted 100 percent extraphysical awareness, I needed to develop much greater maturity, both intra- and extra-physically. This remains an ongoing quest.

The final projection I will recount was in fact one of the last projections I experienced in Brazil. Again, it felt very much like a present, this time a parting present as it happened only a couple of weeks before I was due to return to England. I was taking the second phase of a course in projective techniques at the IIPC's office in Ipanema. The course took place over four consecutive days, and this projection occurred in the last session. Ever since the course began, I had noticed a difference in my nocturnal perceptions, with more lucid projective experiences. I had a sense, based on my subsequent energetic state, of having been projected in previous sessions, but so far I had not had any experiences I could recall. The last lesson involved applying a technique to project with the mentalsoma. There had been three or four students in each of the previous classes, but that day I was the only one to show up.

I did not have any expectations and felt calm, although many thoughts relating to my daily life were running through my mind. During the absorption of energies, the final exercise before starting the technique itself, I felt a lot of activity in the two uppermost chakras, namely the fronto- or 'third-eye' chakra and the crown chakra. They seemed to form a single chakra situated more or less halfway between the two, roughly at the hairline. My head felt like it was heating up from the inside out, with the heat starting from the pineal gland until it focused itself on this midway point between the chakras. This all happened while I was still sitting and working with my energy. When I lay down, that area of my head remained active. The instructor now talked me through a particular muscle relaxation exercise, but once this was over I returned my entire attention to the process that was happening around my head, knowing that it represented the 'entrance' to the mentalsoma.

There was no sense of takeoff whatsoever. It merely felt as if my body disappeared. I found myself in a vast space, or better, it was I who was vastly spacious, expanded. This occurred without any great sense of ecstasy or even the feeling that this experience was in any way special. It simply felt like a change of environment or an improvement in perception. I felt as if I was looking at my intraphysical life from the outside. From here I could see that all the hazards of life and all those events that we might call 'intrusions' are nothing more than energetic phenomena. From this perspective, there was nothing substantial about any of them, and I calmly wondered how they managed to appear so real when I was in the physical body.

I understood that 'I' was not the person who was having the projection of the mentalsoma; rather, 'I' was a mentalsoma who was having the experience of being an intraphysical being. In an inversion of the usual perception, which sees the 'I' going from the intraphysical to engage in extraphysical experiences, I saw that in relation to the infinity of the mentalsoma, any experiences of the personality with which I currently identified were merely ephemeral phenomena.

I attempted to understand how the experiences of the intra-physical consciousness related to this timeless state of the mentalsoma. What, I wondered, was the meaning of physical life? I do not recall coming up with an answer, but there was no urgency to the question while in that state. Unlike the experience we sometimes have in the physical dimension, where we intensely want to understand the purpose of our lives, here it was more idle curiosity that did not carry any major importance.

I had no awareness of 'landing' back in the physical body and no sense of the time that might have passed. When my perception returned to the physical dimension, my body was rigid, my hands were cold, and a ball of hot energy was pulsating at the base of my spine as well as at the top of my head. The crown chakra in particular was distinctly active. I spent another ten minutes or so lying there without moving until the instructor leading the class gave the command to return to physical awareness. The projective experience had lasted 40 to 50 minutes. My mouth was dry, and my body felt both rigid and subtle at the same time.

The experience had an energetic impact that lasted for the next two weeks, during which I felt vibrant with energy and my mind was much calmer than usual. For some days, I could easily re-establish a mental and energetic connection with this projection during my daily life, and when I did so, it produced an increase in my energetic vibrations and a sense of deep contentment. Gradually, this connection faded, and I returned to a more familiar mental and energetic pattern, although I still feel that the experience shifted my sense of self at a very deep level. There have been many occasions over the years when I was caught up in mental or emotional turmoil of one sort or another. At those times, I would think back on that experience and shift my sense of identity beyond my immediate physical reality to that vast and timeless consciousness.

This particular projection also gave me some insight into a problem I had been pondering for a while, namely, why we don't manage to live more by the mentalsoma during our day-to-day lives. In other words, why are we so dominated by the physical body and its many desires (food, sex, addictions) as well as the emotional body and its many neuroses (feelings of insecurity, worthlessness, arrogance, pride and so on)? One possible expla-nation might be the great difference between the reality of the mentalsoma and our intraphysical needs. The perception of the mentalsoma in its pure or naked state without interference from denser energies is so far removed from the needs of our daily existence that bringing it into our lives would have to be learned bit by bit. To put it differently, the intraphysical consciousness must gently and gradually get to know its own true reality so that it can maintain an awareness of that reality without alienating itself from its physical life.

It could be said that I left Brazil on a high. I had not mastered the art of continuous consciousness across dimensions, but I think I dealt with a few things that were much more important for me at that point. My year of being immersed in conscientiology certainly did not free me from all the karmic baggage manifesting as everyday neuroses, but I did leave a much more together, self-reliant and energetically integrated person than when I had arrived. My mental and emotional weaknesses were also about to be attacked from a completely different angle, but I did not know that when I packed my bags, heavy from the many new books I had acquired, and headed back to England.

PART 5

ON MY OWN TWO FEET

Chapter 18

Assuming Responsibility

I had moved to Brazil believing I was traveling to my true spiritual home, but it turned out to have only been another stage of the journey. When the time came, I was happy to be returning to England and looking forward to volunteering at the London office of the IIPC. London was such a relaxing change after a year in Rio de Janeiro. What had previously felt like overwhelming chaos now seemed like an orderly and quiet place. Running IIPC activities, however, was a lot tougher than in Brazil. The name Waldo Vieira has no pull in a country where he has hardly even been heard of, and much of the literature on conscientiology is still confined to Portuguese, so there are a number of challenges in presenting its richness to an Anglophone audience. The IIPC 'office' was run by a group of four volunteers, a couple and two men, all from Brazil. It was actually a small one-bedroom flat that housed the couple and served as a teaching venue. Since those humble beginnings, the London office has turned into a thriving hub for conscientiology across many parts of Europe. But I was not to be a part of this. For me, London was only a short stepping-stone to an entirely new chapter in my evolutionary journey: family life!

The start to life in London was in many ways a continuation of life in Brazil. I felt the helpers very directly when I applied for a job as a team secretary. I knew I would get the job the moment I walked through the door of the job agency, because I had seen it all in a projection the night before. I also found perfect accommodation with a friend in central London. But most of all, I enjoyed developing myself as a conscientiology instructor in my native language.

One of my most significant experiences of this period was a

return visit to my native town of Gütersloh in Germany. Since my last visit, a 'New Age' bookshop had opened in town, something quite radical for the conservative little place. The shop happened to be hosting a kind of Mind-Body-Spirit festival at which I got a speaking spot. This was significant to me for a number of reasons, particularly because it seemed like an excellent opportunity to balance some of my own energetic or thosenic 'footprints' left in that town during my teens and early twenties. Much of that period of my life had involved excessive drug and alcohol use, negative thoughts about myself and others, and occasionally actions that left a number of people hurt or upset. I saw this as an opportunity to channel positive energy into this same environment, consciously cleaning up any negative traces I had left behind.

As should be clear by now, the assumption here is that our thosenes are real energetic 'things' which, even if subtle, live on after we have created them and impact on the environment in which they are found. With this in mind, I spent one day walking through my former hometown, past all my old haunts and alleyways, channeling the most positive thosenes I could muster by focusing on the ultimate connectedness of all conscious-nesses. I also focused on taking responsibility for any negative energies I had left in the town, mentally apologizing to any people I had consciously or unconsciously hurt. While my trip to Mexico had been a more instinctive return to reconcile with my own multiexistential past, this journey was a conscious step towards reconciling with a much more recent past, which nonetheless was related to the other through the period of multi-dimensional intrusion I had been subject to during my 'misspent' youth.

The following day I gave the talk at the Mind-Body-Spirit fair. It was a standard introduction to conscientiology, explaining how projections of consciousness and different energies relate to us as multidimensional beings, in addition to encouraging people to experiment, seek experiences, and be wary of belief systems. Despite having given this talk numerous times before, I was so nervous I had to deliver it sitting down, as I was unsure whether my legs would support me. Even the very tangible presence of extraphysical helpers could not alleviate this condition. Both my nervousness and the energies I was experiencing were intense. While fear of public speaking is very common (some claim that many of us fear public speaking more than death!), the extent of it was out of the ordinary for me, and I attribute this intensity to energetic resistance and attempts at intrusion by extraphysical consciousnesses. That night, I felt utterly exhausted but also very peaceful. I knew I had cleared up at least some of the energetic history and negative groupkarmic links I had left in that place.

I enjoyed this and other opportunities to teach conscientiology and felt very much in sync with my life purpose in this respect. But at the same time, I became increasingly aware of the lack of a partner in my life. Unlike many spiritual traditions that advocate a life of celibacy, conscientiology emphasizes the need to find a partner with whom we can form what is called an 'evolutionary duo'. An evolutionary duo is a partnership between two people who share their intraphysical lives much like a conventional relationship, but in addition both are committed to supporting each other in their evolution and contributing to some form of assistance to others, thereby advancing the evolution of consciousness more broadly.

Beyond this lofty ideal though, one strong driving force for my desire to find a partner was definitely sex! I had been without a partner for some time, and my basic sexual needs were not being satisfied. Sexual energy is a very powerful force, and a strong sexual relationship is an important feature of an evolutionary duo. Energetically speaking, if our sexual energies are out of balance, our whole energetic system is vulnerable to intrusion. I received a sobering lesson on the possible extent of this when the lady in whose apartment I was living in London introduced me to a young woman. My host was clearly seeking to match make us. It was true that the young woman was delightful, but we were definitely not on the same wavelength. Nonetheless, we did meet a few times, and on one of these occasions, her pert bottom caught my attention as she walked ahead of me. There was an immediate energetic charge that seemed to jump from her backside to my groin area, and my penis began to sting. This condition persisted, and after a couple of days, I visited a health clinic where I was diagnosed with a urinary tract infection and prescribed antibiotics. It seemed that I had caught an infection purely through energy! I had been vulnerable to this, because of the imbalance in my own sexual energies. An evolutionary duo that practices regular mutually satisfying sex provides an ideal preventive measure against this kind of vulnerability, as well as against the risk of sexual encounters with energetically hungry extraphysical consciousnesses outside of the body. During semi-conscious or unconscious projections, we often seek to fulfill our own basic unmet needs and we can easily attract extraphysical consciousnesses who still thrive on the sexual energies of the human body. If such encounters are recalled at all, it is usually just as 'erotic dreams', but because the extraphysical conscious-nesses involved are generally not healthy, they can have very real repercussions on our level of energy and the clarity of our thosenes. In other words, by providing the basis for a healthy energetic equilibrium, a close sexual relationship can help both partners to focus on more productive multidimensional endeavors. But an evolutionary duo is about a lot more than sex, and I was very clear that I did not just want to find a temporary relationship to satisfy that desire. I had been down that road in the past and knew that I wanted something more. I wanted to share my life's journey with someone.

In spite of these thoughts, establishing an evolutionary duo was not what I had in mind when I headed to Australia to meet my son and his mother. You may have noticed that so far I have only made a passing mention of my son's birth. This reflects the fact that up until this point I had been too busy focusing on my own multidimensional experiences. I had not appreciated the significant responsibility that comes with fathering a child. Fortunately, my mother knew something about this and encouraged me to meet my son for his first birthday. I was immediately besotted with the chubby, smiley, cheeky little person I met, but it took me a while to work out what this meant in practical terms. After spending an intense period of almost three years in which I thought that the rest of my life would be focused on multidimensional learning and teaching, I suddenly realized that I needed to attend to intraphysical responsibilities. Initially, I toyed with the idea of being a long-distance father. Naively, I thought I would be able to maintain a relationship with my son from overseas. Fortunately, I went to see a family counselor. She informed me that it was very common for parents to relate to their children in the same way that they themselves had been related to. This can even include developing similar behaviors or changing the relationship when the child turns the same age they were when their parents made the same changes. It was clearly another case of mimicry, but this time, it was inter-generational mimicry. When I was growing up, my father had been in another country, and I had not had a child–parent relationship with him. I did not want to perpetuate that pattern. Eventually, I left Australia, having agreed with the woman who is now my wife not only to share in raising our son but also to live together as partners. Some months later, she and our son joined me in England, and the family adventure began.

Chapter 19

Different Evolutionary Paths

An intimate relationship can provide an excellent space for personal development, being both challenging and rewarding. How do I bring my own needs, desires and priorities into a partnership with another person whose focus may be very different from mine? My way of going through life up to this point had been largely by myself, so I could really do as I pleased. Now I needed to learn how to stay true to myself while living in a respectful and loving relationship. My new wife and I both shared a passion for personal growth and an experience of consciousness as multidimensional, but we discovered fairly quickly that we pursued these things quite differently.

Early on in our relationship, my wife met Amma. Amma, or Sri Mata Amritanandamayi Devi in full, is an Indian holy woman or *satguru*. She has become known as 'the hugging saint' because during her gatherings she hugs everyone who attends, ostensibly to bestow her blessing on them. Thousands of people come to see her as she travels across the world to raise money for her charitable activities, and she has been known to hug people for more than 20 hours straight without food or a bathroom break, beaming smiles and with focused attention the entire time.

While we were living in Geneva, Switzerland, my wife saw a poster of Amma, advertising one of her events in Italy. There was no question: she was going. I could relate well to this kind of urgency, even if I did not respond to Amma in the same way. After we moved to Australia, we learned that Amma held regular retreats here. It had not been that long ago that I too had attended events with guru-like figures. Before going to Brazil, I had attended a Buddhist retreat in northern England, where one of the main teachings had been to put one's trust in the principal teacher who would assist the devoted disciple to move from illusion to enlightenment. This is the classic structure of the Eastern traditions: a few people blaze the trail that the masses can follow. They are the gurus, and if we follow their advice and, perhaps more importantly, link to their energies, we too can achieve liberation or enlightenment.

This structure never sat well with me. Even at the Buddhist retreat, where we were encouraged to focus our minds on the guru, I would focus on the abstract notion of pure consciousness. My resistance to this approach to spiritual life had only been strengthened through my studies of conscientiology, which strongly argues against any guru worship as a form of dependence and an abdication of personal responsibility. So when my wife wanted us all to attend the Amma retreat, I was resistant. If she wanted to go, that was OK, but I would not be coming. She wanted our young child to experience the presence of Amma, but she also wanted to have some freedom to take full advantage of the retreat. So I traveled with her, but I did not enter the retreat. I spent time with my son outside, and occasionally he would go into the hall with his mother.

To cut a long story short, over the years my position softened. I have now attended many Amma retreats and been hugged by her many times. Her hugs can be intense experiences, energetically cleansing and uplifting. I have seen her give generously, tirelessly and lovingly of herself to all who come to her. There is no discrimination or prerequisite for people to come and experience profound love. She is a multidimensional epicenter of extensive proportions and at any single time is assisting not only intraphysical but also extraphysical consciousnesses. The atmosphere at her events is usually mildly euphoric, with people experiencing spontaneous expansions of consciousness and a reduction in intrusion.

Over the years, I have grappled with the question of why a consciousness who is clearly extremely lucid would perpetuate the classic pattern of assuming a god-like position, allowing herself to be worshiped in the way that Amma does, or maintain some of the more conservative and restricted dogmas of classical Indian religion with regard to sex or diet. The assumption that underpins this questioning is that a consciousness like the one manifesting as Amma is so lucid that she consciously chooses the way she manifests and that creating an environment in which everything about her is worshiped by her disciples is not due to her being caught in old karmic patterns or some kind of ego-trip masquerading as spirituality, but a deliberate action motivated by a deep desire to be of service to others. I now think the answer is fairly straightforward. The guru–disciple relationship has a strong historical precedent, as does the idea of an 'enlightened master'. It is socially accepted not just in the East but also increasingly in the West and will have played a role in previous existences for many of us. This means that people who may find it more difficult to connect with more abstract or independent forms of multidimensional assistance can relate to, feel comfortable with and find support in this framework. Amma's focus on charitable works and her willingness to embrace anybody who comes to her maximizes her social and human connections and allows anybody to have a taste of the multidi-mensional energy we call 'love'. Unlike an intellectual discipline like conscientiology, people are not required to think or work anything out before receiving their dose of energy. Over the years, I have moved from a position of judging the process around Amma as essentially negative, because it seemed to foster dependence and reduce personal responsibility, to seeing it as profoundly assistential. While there are aspects of that process that do not resonate well with me personally, I have seen and experienced the energetic benefits generated by Amma, and I have come to appreciate that her processes are exactly what works for many people.

The driving force behind Amma is the same force that I saw

in Waldo Vieira, Leia, Pak Suyono and many extraphysical helpers: 'love' seems to be the best word we have for it in this dimension. From the perspective of love, all those people are playing equally important parts in the vast process of assistance that is propelling the evolution of consciousness across dimensions, both on this planet and beyond.

Chapter 20

The Multidimensional Evolution of Consciousness

This book has specifically focused on four intense years of my life, starting with my visit to Shanti Loka in 1995 and ending with my step into family life in 1999. It was a period during which my worldview was first shattered and then gradually reassembled. I feel very fortunate to have met the three teachers I introduced in this book. Together they provided me with all the tools and assistance I needed to develop my understanding of our lives as multidimensional consciousnesses. Pak Suyono introduced me to the power of mindfulness, and being aware of the body continues to be a simple but effective technique for bringing presence to any situation. Leia infused me with a high dose of energy that gave me access to layers of myself I had previously ignored and helped me not to get stuck in old patterns. Finally, Waldo Vieira provided the intellectual framework that gave my experiences a coherent and lucid context.

Since leaving Brazil, I have essentially no longer had a direct teacher or someone I looked towards for guidance or information. That is not to say that I felt that I now knew it all or that I was not in need of support; far from it. I have continued studying and learning from many people since then, but I no longer focus on one particular individual for guidance. As I make my way through life, I have tried to remain connected with and true to my multidimensional reality while assuming family, professional and social responsibilities. But while I have continued to study a range of psycho-spiritual systems for the variety of insights they offer, conscientiology has provided me with a consistent personal reference point. I will therefore conclude this book by pulling together the key understandings I have gained from that discipline, about how the many experiences I have described relate to the multidimensional evolution of consciousness.

This book has focused on a period of my life that was marked by many multidimensional phenomena and peak experiences. The phenomena have not stopped; after all, they are a natural part of human life. But it has been quite a while since I have had experiences like the ones Leia induced. The period during which I associated with her felt like one long peak experience. Yet over the years, I have come to appreciate that we can become 'experience junkies'. In other words, it is very tempting to pursue experiences for their own sake. After all, it feels great to enter an exalted state of consciousness or explore extraphysical dimensions. But then what?

What I realized when I moved into the role of father and family man was that none of my many peak experiences had prepared me for that task. Probably what prepared me most was the energetic development I enjoyed as a result of managing life in Rio de Janeiro. Some of the peak experiences, such as the mentalsomatic projection (see Chapter 17), helped me in the sense that they profoundly altered my perspective on life. When the stress of limited finances and incessant family demands seemed overwhelming, connecting with the sense of my true nature as immortal consciousness could really pick me up and help me to focus on transcendental love, a force that always puts other issues into perspective. The circumstances of family life, however, required me to develop certain inner muscles that none of my teachers or experiences of consciousness had taught me. The natural immaturities of my children triggered my own immaturities and forced me to overcome them. I also had to let go of idealized expectations and personal desires as my kids grew into their very own personalities. And negotiating, maintaining and growing an intimate relationship in the midst of ceaseless demands for time and energy by children, domestic dross and financial necessities is a challenge most parents are only too aware of. This, too, was of indispensable evolutionary value.

This is not to discount my peak experiences. Some were essential for my energetic healing and growth while others left me with a much clearer understanding of the evolutionary journey of consciousness and allowed me to approach life with a sense of equanimity. The point is that our evolution is a highly complex and multifaceted process. For many of us, it involves pursuing multidimensional experiences that help us connect with our extraphysical reality, because it is from that reality that we originate and it is there that we are really ourselves. But if we pursue such experiences at the expense of our intraphysical responsibilities and commitments, we are neglecting important aspects of ourselves. And if we pursue them simply because they make us feel better, we are missing the essential ingredient of evolution: assisting others. As Pak Suyono said, the era of monks and gurus is coming to an end, and we are now in a time where consciousnesses will pursue evolution through self-directed and multifaceted avenues while living a productive intraphysical life with partners, families and gainful endeavors.

Extraterrestrial Life

My experiences have made it very clear to me that the evolution of consciousness is multidimensional and occurs on a timescale that is almost impossible for humans to grasp. We are all older than this planet. We have all been on other planets. And there are many people with non-human bodies arriving from other planets all the time. These different bodies are as incidental to our evolution as are the different races of humans. Just because a consciousness is currently manifesting in a body that has allowed it to travel through space and time in ways unknown to humans does not mean that the consciousness occupying that body is superior to the consciousnesses occupying human bodies. Once the ET 'dies', or deactivates that particular body of physical manifestation and then activates its human body, he or she will be subject to all the same limitations that characterize long-term humans right now, maybe even more so as he or she grapples with the workings of the new vehicle.

At this stage, much of humanity is still struggling to live together in acceptance of racial and cultural differences. I believe that we are greatly improving our track record in that regard as a result of both globalization and the arrival of an increasing number of more lucid consciousnesses in this dimension. It will be some time, though, before we are able to coexist in a mature way with consciousnesses manifesting in extraterrestrial bodies. Until then, our interactions with extraterrestials may largely remain at the extraphysical level.

Hallucinogenic Drugs

Another thing I have learned over the years is that the expansion of our awareness is a gradual process that goes hand in hand with the expansion of our energetic condition. Our energetic level increases through persistent practice of particular techniques, for example, the closed circulation technique described in this book. Major peak experiences, such as projections with the mentalsoma, can also dramatically raise our vibrational frequency, even if only temporarily, and give us glimpses of the kind of awareness that is possible. To reach those states on an ongoing basis, we need to gradually increase our vibrational frequency and intensity.

Early in the book, I described my peyote experience, and I think it is worth commenting briefly on the use of such drugs, which remain an easy and quite popular way to seek peak experiences. We generally refer to them as hallucinogens, based on the assumption that they induce hallucinations. Some people refer to them as entheogens because they feel that the drugs connect them with an aspect of the divine. From the perspective of conscientiology, they are most accurately described as projectiogens, because they induce projections of consciousness and thereby give access to extraphysical dimensions. There are many different types of these drugs, including: ayahuasca, DMT, iboga, LSD, peyote and psilocybin mushrooms. Many of them have traditionally been used in religious and transformative ceremonies, and some have been adopted as regular tools for spiritual exploration in Western society as well. Based on my experiences, I have come to the view that these drugs somehow affect all our multidimensional bodies, altering the energosoma and causing partial or total projections of either the psychosoma or mentalsoma. By doing so they give us access to insights and perceptions of other dimensions, often positive but sometimes disturbing and psychologically detrimental, depending on our own holothosene.

During the time that I was regularly seeing Leia, I recall a friend commenting that I looked as if I were permanently on acid (LSD). I was not, in fact, taking drugs of any kind, but the expansions of consciousness I experienced naturally during that period were reminiscent of states experienced on projectiogenic drugs; or perhaps it would be more accurate to say that the experiences people have on drugs are reminiscent of those we can enjoy without drugs when the energies are right.

Projectiogenic drugs can induce expansions and even projections of the mentalsoma that lead to profound perceptions. They can produce life-changing insights and encourage takers to reprioritize their lives in more beneficial ways. They do, however, also pose significant risks. There is always the risk of a consciousness having a 'bad trip', or rather, a bad projection involving major intrusion that can lead to temporary or permanent mental imbalance. Equally significant is the impact the long-term use of such drugs can have on a person's energetic system. From an energetic perspective, the drugs function like rockets, blasting us up to peak levels without any effort on our own part. This very easily leads to a psychological dependence, as we crave the peak experience but do not have the independent energetic muscle to reach it by ourselves. So we revert to the drug. But what is the drug doing to our energetic system? I once overheard Leia speaking to a young man who regularly took LSD and psilocybin mushrooms. She suggested that drugs like that might show us some aspects of our true nature but that if we take them too often, they may make it impossible for us to actually reach a permanent awareness of our multidimensional reality by ourselves. On reflection, my understanding now is that such drugs may ultimately impact on our so-called kundalini energy, the energy which moves from our base chakra to our crown chakra, in such a way that we cannot actually raise our frequency on a permanent basis or reach mentalsomatic projections by ourselves anymore.

One of the key lessons in pursuing multidimensional awareness over an extended period of time has been the need for balance. Even if our perspective on life is purely physical, we realize that we need to balance physical activity, diet, work, leisure time and so on. Once we add energy work, a psychosoma and mentalsoma, multidimensional awareness, karmic responsibilities, assistential tasks and goals that go beyond this current physical lifetime, there are many more things to balance, and this includes the way in which we pursue peak experiences.

The Existential Program

One way of looking at the evolution of consciousness is that it moves ahead in units we call 'lifetimes'. Each of our physical lives is a new chapter in the journey, and with each physical lifetime, we start with a new game plan and a new set of targets and goals to achieve. In conscientiology, we call this game plan our 'existential program'. This existential program is what we designed during our intermissive period prior to this current life, when our awareness was greater and we had a clearer perspective of where we came from and what we wanted to accomplish in the next physical life. We all have an existential program that is tailor-made to our circumstances, needs and abilities, and whatever your existential program may be, it is perfectly achievable by you.

In my case, the existential program for this life involves first understanding multidimensionality better for myself and then helping others to understand it. There was a risk that I would deviate from this part of my program and restrict my understanding to more conventional religious systems because of my deep karmic connections with them. There was probably a risk that I wouldn't even get that far and end up spending this life largely dealing with drug and alcohol issues. Fortunately, I managed to avoid both of those pitfalls, thanks to significant assistance from the helpers. My existential program also involved having a family. Just because we have a family, though, does not mean that this is necessarily our existential program. For some people, family life may actually be self-mimicry and a deviation from the program they had set themselves, while for others, it is a central part of their life plan. In my case, taking responsibility for a family seems to be an important evolutionary opportunity at this point in my journey.

The important thing to remember is that our existential programs are highly personal. What is right for one person may not be right for the next. We really need to go into ourselves and find our own answers for what is right for each of us. But there are some key principles that generally apply. Our existential program will involve overcoming or transforming at least some of our weak traits. These are aspects of ourselves that we have neglected in our evolutionary journeys so far and that we now need to address. In my case, this includes being closely and intimately involved with other people, such as my family. In most of my retrocognitions, I saw myself as somewhat detached from others: aloof, distant, self-absorbed, sometimes downright cruel. In this lifetime, it has taken ongoing work both by me and my partner to maintain my emotional and mental presence within the relationship and my family life. That is my story. The things you will need to address will be different.

Another aspect of our existential programs, to one degree or another, is making a difference in the lives of others. Again, how this looks in practice will be highly individual. Just consider the contributions of the three main teachers I discuss in this book. For Waldo, helping others has meant creating landmark publications and innovative methodologies that have given rise to new ways of understanding and conceptualizing consciousness, and then establishing organizations through which to make this under-standing available around the world. Leia and Pak Suyono have made less obvious of an external impact, but all three have provided direct assistance through words and energies both within and outside the body to countless numbers of people. Then there are people like Mandela and Gandhi, whose actions changed the course of nations, or like Rosa Parks, whose refusal to move to the back of the bus heralded the end of racial segre-gation in the USA. But actions do not have to be on that scale. For one person, raising children in a loving and supportive family home may be the main focus; for another, it might be bringing neighbors together in communal action or working with disad-vantaged youth, the elderly, indigenous peoples or some other group of people in need of support. The scale and nature of our work is highly personal, but some form of reaching out beyond our individual egos to support other evolving consciousnesses will be an aspect of our existential program. Again, for some running a soup kitchen for homeless people might be part of their existential program, while for others that would be a deviation from their program, because really their task was the creation of high-level policies or systems aimed at addressing the more fundamental causes of homelessness. Only you and your helpers can know what is right for you and what is an accommodation or even a downright deviation.

Our existential programs are unlikely to involve Hollywood-style heroics, but they will involve a kind of internal heroism, of confronting ourselves and standing up for things we believe are important, even if they challenge general community standards or social expectations. There is really nothing more important in our physical lives than completing our existential program. It is the whole point of why we are here. When we eventually deactivate our current bodies, we alone will be measuring our own success. There will be no external judgment. We will judge ourselves, and we will naturally respond by either feeling very content with our achievements or by being deeply frustrated and unhappy at a job poorly done.

It is not hard to relate this to our everyday experiences. Think of how you feel when you are aware of things that you need to do but so far have left undone. You procrastinate over your university assignments; you have been out of touch with your parents or old friends for much too long; every time you walk past your shed, you get a sinking feeling because you have been meaning to tidy it up for the past two years. What might start with a subtle sense of gnawing dissatisfaction can easily grow into negative self-talk and a sense of frustration. Contrast this with how you feel after you have completed something. Imagine that you have finished setting up a new website for your business, renovated your house, or handed in your final assignment. In my experience, there is an inner sense of satisfaction, and if it was something really important, even passing euphoria. Now multiply those feelings a hundredfold. If we complete our life task, we are content, euphoric even, on a profound inner level. If we don't, we become depressed, melancholy, and regretful. Those states of mind will then accompany us beyond this current life, and will not only influence our subsequent experience of the extraphysical dimension but can also impact on our next intraphysical existence. And self-mimicry applies even here! All the choices and habits that led us to not complete our existential program in one lifetime are just as likely to catch up with us again, as are the choices and habits that helped us to complete our program.

If a physical lifetime is a unit in the evolution of consciousness, a day is a unit in the execution of our existential program. The only time to adjust our course and make sure that we are on track is *now*, the most fundamental evolutionary moment of all. Right now is the time to work with energy, to learn something new, to deepen our understanding through research and writing, to make sure we address something we have left undone, to confront an inner weakness or make a difference in the life of another. If we do all we can every day, we can be sure to leave this life with a smile on our face.

Karma

Most of us have heard about karma. But what does it really mean? Sometimes people think it is the same thing as 'destiny', that we have no choice in certain matters because our karma will dictate what happens. I have come to understand karma as a dynamic force. It is the law of cause and effect, and it includes dynamics that we set in motion a long time ago, literally lifetimes ago, that will affect us now. As long as we are unconscious of these dynamics, they are indeed somewhat like destiny. For example, I struggled with drugs and alcohol and suffered what for me was inexplicable mental confusion as a young man. This was the result of a particular karmic debt. Had this continued and seriously impacted my life, it might have seemed like a 'bad destiny'. But once I became aware of myself and my own dynamic, I was able to transform the process. So this is the key point: karma is created at every moment, and at every moment, we have the opportunity to change our 'destiny'.

In conscientiology, we try to understand karma in a more nuanced way. Waldo has developed different conceptual categories of karma: egokarma, groupkarma and polykarma. The first two are probably relatively self-explanatory. Egokarma is what concerns us as individuals: our sense of self, our ability to look after our own mental, emotional and physical well-being; basically, our ability to live well in our own skin and 'paraskin'. Groupkarma concerns our relationships with our karmic group. This group is much larger than we might think at first. Naturally, it includes our family, friends, work colleagues, schoolmates and so on. But it also includes many people who are currently not in the physical dimension or people we have not physically met in this lifetime but with whom we have close evolutionary ties. Our relationships with consciousnesses from this group can take many forms. Some may be characterized by great affection, others may leave us rather hoping that we don't see the person again, while still others may be indifferent. It is worth considering where we are positioned in evolutionary terms within our group. Have we caused others harm or assisted them? Are we more of a helper or do we more often receive help? Or are we perhaps a blind guide, well meaning but leading our friends astray as far as their own evolutionary journey is concerned? The consciousness who was attached to me in response to my past actions is part of my karmic group, as are my old drinking buddies, my parents and siblings, wife and children, as well as Waldo, Leia, Pak Suyono and my extraphysical helpers. Clearly, it is a diverse group. Finally, polykarma is our karma with respect to all consciousnesses in the cosmos at large, human and non-human, physical and extraphysical, in all dimensions.

We can think of ourselves as having three karmic accounts. We will all have an active balance sheet for the first two. The egokarmic and groupkarmic accounts are active simply by the very nature of our existence, as every consciousness is interdependent with others. The more self-absorbed we are, the greater the focus will be on our egokarmic account, but even the most self-absorbed person is in relationship with others. We can think of our actions as causing either credits or debits to our karmic accounts. Suicide victims create a debit both in their egokarmic account and in their groupkarmic account through the pain and suffering they cause others. The philanthropist may be accumulating groupkarmic credits but may still struggle with egokarmic issues such as maintaining a healthy physical body. The polykarmic account may not necessarily be active at this stage as long as our manifestations are largely focused on ourselves (egokarma) and those more prominent in our life (groupkarma). When we start making positive contributions to our polykarmic account, we will be operating at a level of assistance beyond race, religion or gender and from an awareness that the consciousnesses who are the perpetrators of the suffering of others are in just as much need of assistance as those who are their victims.

From a personal perspective on the evolutionary trajectory of this life, I needed to sort out basic egokarmic business before I was in a state where I could meaningfully engage with the practices and information made available to me through Pak Suyono, Leia, Waldo and others. These practices in turn enabled me to increase both my awareness and my active contribution to my group- and polykarmic accounts. So one way of thinking about evolution is as a trajectory that might begin with debits in our ego- and groupkarmic accounts but that ends, after many lifetimes, with a great surplus in all our accounts, including our polykarmic account as we provide ever greater levels of indiscriminate assistance to all consciousnesses.

The Journey to Freedom from Intrusion

Another way of thinking about the evolutionary journey is as movement from a condition where I experience regular intrusion to a condition of complete freedom from intrusion. As you will recall, intrusion refers to the experience in which our mental or emotional state is temporarily altered by the pathological energies of another consciousness. Unless you are in a very small percentage of the world's population, you will experience intrusion from time to time, and one significant goal we can have for this lifetime is to reach the state of being permanently and totally intrusion-free. This is a condition of profound mental, emotional and energetic equilibrium where we are no longer subject to even the most occasional moment of intrusion.

Peak experiences are an inevitable part of our movement towards that state as we open up our energetic pathways and gain greater self-understanding through retrocognitions and other multidimensional experiences. But they are only one aspect. A focus on multidimensional service is the key driver. It is by being of service, both physically and on a multidimensional level, that we extend ourselves beyond our limited egokarma and gradually open the universal polykarmic account that relates to our connection with consciousnesses at all levels of manifestation. It is by going beyond our own egos that we are confronted with the shortcomings that open us up to intrusion in the first place.

As long as we are subject to intrusion, our ride will be rocky. We advance a few steps but are then taken on a detour through some rough emotional terrain or spend extended periods in a barren mental wilderness. Being permanently and totally intrusion-free is not the end of the road. It is not enlightenment or nirvana. Rather, it is the beginning of the period where we can take conscious and deliberate evolutionary actions without continuous interference. When we are in that state, we are finally at our most efficient in terms of providing assistential energies to those around us in all dimensions. We are not perfect. We will still have weaknesses to improve and skills to learn, but we can now do things so much more freely and rapidly. It is also a state that, once achieved, will be ours to keep, an evolutionary conquest across lifetimes. Consequently, this should be our next evolutionary goal, right now in this lifetime, so that we can transform our journey forever.

How do we achieve this goal? In the abstract, the answer is simple: work with your energy and your thosenes (thoughts and emotions) to eliminate any sources of self-intrusion (i.e. fostering obsessive or pathological thosenes); be disciplined with all your bodies, including the physical; be rigorous in your self-analysis and identification of weak traits and mini-pathologies; be of service to others; and always remember love! In concrete terms, the journey to freedom from intrusion will be just as unique for every one of us as our individual evolutionary journeys up to this point. For some of us our family dynamics may provide the perfect space to overcome intrusions, for others it may be our work environment, and in many cases our engagement in some evolutionary endeavor will play a significant role in assisting us on the path to totally and permanently overcoming intrusion. This is not something distant or unobtainable; it is a realistic and significant goal for this very life.

Enlightenment

Given that many spiritual traditions have a notion of enlightenment as the ultimate goal of our evolutionary journey, I thought I would end with a few words on this concept. None of my teachers ever talked about this idea or suggested that there was an end to evolution. Leia suggested that Linda had completed her last physical existence when she vacated her body for Leia, but there was no suggestion that she would now retire into some form of cosmic bliss. In fact, she seemed to be very busy as a member of the Boardroom. In conscientiology, we understand that there comes a time when consciousnesses no longer have the need for intraphysical existences. When we reach that point, we will have mastered energies to such a level that we now need to move on to the subtle dimensions of the mentalsoma for new and more expanded evolutionary challenges beyond our current comprehension. People who get to that stage, the *Homo Sapiens Serenissimus*, have been intrusion-free for many lifetimes and have provided increasingly significant levels of assistance across the planet and all extraphysical dimensions. We do not achieve this condition in one lifetime.

My experience in this lifetime has been that, rather than achieving new or previously unexplored levels of awareness, most of the evolutionary dynamic seems to be aimed at trying to regain an awareness we already enjoy when we are extraphysical. In other words, as we work towards increasing our multidimensional awareness, we are really just working at becoming more of ourselves, at bringing more of our original self into this dimension. Conscientiology has developed a useful way of thinking about this. According to this model we all have 1000 units of lucidity, which represent our full level of awareness. These units are called 'cons'. When we are between physical lives, and assuming we are healthy and manifesting only in our psychosoma (with nothing left over from the energetic body) in a subtle extraphysical dimension, we enjoy full awareness, expressing all our 1000 units of lucidity. The 1000 cons are a personal measure. Your awareness at 1000 cons may look different from mine or your next-door neighbor's. The point is that we all have a peak state of awareness.

When we reactivate a new physical body, this awareness becomes restricted. We could say that when we are newly born, we have one con. Gradually, as we grow and mature, we regain our units of awareness. Because of the limits of our physical bodies, none of us, with the possible exception of the *Homo Sapiens Serenissimus*, will recuperate the full 1000 cons in the physical dimension; but if we regain more than half of our extraphysical awareness, we will be doing quite well. When we feel that the knowledge and answers are within us or that certain expanded states of consciousness seem extremely familiar and welcoming, we are right. We are actually just returning to a state that is more natural to us than the limitations of the physical body.

Against this understanding, the concept of 'enlightenment', at least in the simplistic sense of achieving some kind of ultimate state of consciousness that represents the end of our evolutionary journey, is simply not helpful to me. In one lifetime, the evolutionary journey involves expanded states of consciousness and increases in awareness that are largely a reclaiming of our own cons, our own lucidity. But over time we are also increasing both our capacity to recuperate cons while in the physical dimension and the overall lucidity that our 1000 cons represent.

As mentioned above, the attainment of total and permanent freedom from intrusion is an evolutionary conquest that will allow us to enjoy a previously unknown state of peace and equanimity. But it, too, is just another stage of ever increasing awareness and energetic control, the ultimate extent of which is unfathomable for many of us right now. Yet it is where we are all headed. There is no end to that growth as far as I can see. Even once we leave the physical dimension altogether, we will simply start a new evolutionary chapter in the mental dimension.

And as with any long journey, the most important point is where we are right here and now. This is the time when we influence the next steps and stages, right now, by our thoughts, emotions and actions. This is a great time to have a physical body. The opportunities to travel the world offered in our current time, both physically and virtually (online) are unprecedented, and they allow us to reconnect with many more evolutionary colleagues than we would ever have been able to in previous lifetimes. Despite the fact that the world is experiencing significant threats and challenges to the well-being of the human race, this is a very privileged time to be in this dimension, as we can clear groupkarmic debts and add to our polykarmic account like never before. Let's make the most of this evolutionary opportunity and put in place a pattern of completing our existential programs that we will carry with us for our future intraphysical lives. The time is now!

Epilogue

The Nameless Teacher

This book has largely been about the three people who have played key roles in guiding and assisting me and many others. The importance of teachers in our multidimensional evolutionary journeys is traditionally taken as a given. In the classic traditions of the East, the guru–disciple relationship is a philosophical cornerstone. Interestingly, none of my teachers endorsed a dynamic in which there was any kind of dependency on them by me or any other 'students'. Pak Suyono spoke of the end of the era of gurus and distanced himself from any transformations the people around him might have been experiencing. Leia took active measures to push people away after the benefit of the intraphysical contact with her had run its course. And Waldo Vieira militates against any guru-worship or any form of relationship that undermines a person's energetic and mental independence. All of them, though, were teachers who provided information and instructions in certain techniques as well as energetic assistance to people who came to them.

Then there are those teachers who don't teach in the classical sense at all, but who simply alter us through their energies and their ability to impact our mental and emotional state. I met one such person, although I never got to know him and we only had two interactions. From a superficial perspective, there is no reason to assume that this person influenced my life in any way. Yet, when I think of this man, I regularly experience energetic showers and deep, spontaneous emotions of affection and gratitude.

I met him in the summer of 1995 in Sanary-sur-Mer, southern France, where my girlfriend at the time and I had a hair-wrapping stall. He was stretched out on the seafront promenade, ostensibly begging for money. Tall, bearded and wearing shabby clothes, he exuded an air more like a 19th-century traveler than a 20th-century *clochard*, or homeless person. He radiated an inexplicable calm, lying there propped up on one elbow. His hat was placed a good ten meters away from him, and he seemed completely detached from it, as if it did not really matter to him whether he got any money. I noticed him from afar and realized that I would be passing by his hat. Immediately my mind erupted in a mental debate, with one part feeling obliged to give him money while another reminded me earnestly of who I was: a poor hair-wrapper trying to make a meager holiday living with his girlfriend. So, no, I decided, I did not have to give this man anything. As I walked past his hat with my mind in this strange turmoil, it was as though something pulled me back, and I did something I had never done before. I turned around to put some money in his hat. I stuck my hand in my pocket and came up with a 20 franc piece. 'No, too much!' the imaginary hair-wrapper cried, and I ended up throwing a few smaller coins in his hat. *'Merci, jeune homme'* (Thanks, young man), he said in a deep, calm voice without moving from his reclining position.

That same evening as I was frantically wrapping hair at the busy seaside market, I noticed him striding through the crowd, and as I did, his presence seemed to penetrate my being with a sensation I had never experienced before. At the end of the evening, I discovered that the 20 francs piece had disappeared. I cannot be entirely certain that I did not accidentally give it out as 10 francs change to a customer (the two coins looked fairly similar), but the significance, in any event, was not that the money disappeared. To me, that was just a form of communication, a way of making sure I really noticed. The significance was the energetic exchange.

For some reason, this highly evolved consciousness (for that is what I now think he was) entered my life at a time of major inner and outer change. I am still not fully aware of the impact this encounter had on my ability to make the transformations I was soon to make, but I feel certain that it was significant. This anonymous man may well have given me the added energetic and thosenic boost I needed not to become distracted when, some weeks after this event, I would be trying to understand why I was leaving my girlfriend for an unknown meditation center in Indonesia. Without this silent intervention, who knows how this story would have looked?

Glossary

assistential – the quality of being of assistance to others often from a multidimensional perspective. For example, a person can have assistential energy, or helpers are engaged in assistential activities.

baratrosphere – the densest extraphysical dimension, consisting of communities of pathological consciousnesses, ignorant of their condition and caught in all manner of mental and emotional illusions and suffering. Synonyms: barathrum, gehenna, hell, hell realms, limbo, naraka, tartarus.

bioenergy (bio + energy) – the 'energy of life'. A subtle form of energy that animates all living things and constitutes the energosoma of the human being. Synonyms: Chi, Ki, Prana, Qui.

blind guide – a well-meaning extraphysical consciousness of limited awareness and lacking an inner sense of morality and ethics. Will lead us off our ideal evolutionary trajectory despite acting with the best of intentions.

chakra – a vortex of energy in our energosoma. If healthy, our chakras will be spinning and distributing energy throughout our holosoma.

con – a hypothetical unit of lucidity. The con provides an individual measure; every consciousness has 1000 cons when fully lucid and in a healthy extraphysical state. Every time we reactivate a new physical body our lucidity is greatly reduced, and part of our evolutionary challenge is to regain as many cons as we can in each physical lifetime.

consciential – of or pertaining to the consciousness.

consciential assistance – actions of a helper or an intraphysical consciousness who benefits one or more intraphysical consciousnesses through therapeutic energies or illuminating thosenes.

consciential energy – the energy that is produced when immanent energy is molded or formatted through the thoughts and emotions of a consciousness.

consciential epicenter – a lucid intraphysical consciousness who provides consistent interdimensional energetic assistance and has established an extraphysical office as a result. Directly related to Penta.

consciential intrusion – the negative influence, experienced by an intraphysical consciousness, of disturbed thosenes emitted consciously or unconsciously by one or more extraphysical consciousness. Extreme cases can include outright possession, but more commonly manifested through temporary or chronic mental, emotional, energetic and physical disturbances.

consciential self-mimicry – unnecessary repetitions in this lifetime of actions and life-choices from previous lives, leading to evolutionary stagnation.

conscientiology – the science that studies the consciousness in an experiential and integral way, including all the multidimensional, holosomatic and multiexistential manifestations of consciousness and all types of parapsychic phenomena.

coronochakra – the chakra located at the apex of our skull, most directly related to the mentalsoma and expansions of consciousness.

cosmic consciousness – a state of consciousness induced through a full or partial projection of the mentalsoma, in which the consciousness feels itself transcending its usual individual identity and connected to the entire multidimensional cosmos. Often ineffable. Also cosmoconsciousness.

desoma (deactivation + soma) – the process whereby the consciousness leaves its current physical body for the last time and returns to the extraphysical dimension. Commonly known as 'death', this experience represents the final projection of an intraphysical consciousness.

egokarma (ego + karma) – the karma generated by a consciousness with regard to itself. This level of karma dominates when we are more self-absorbed and egocentric. See also groupkarma and polykarma.

energetic epicenter – see consciential epicenter

energosoma (energo + soma) – the energetic body, constituted of innumerable chakras and channels of energy, that permeates and animates the physical body and can be controlled by our will.

epicenter – see consciential epicenter

evolutiologist – a highly evolved consciousness, can be intra- or extraphysical, who facilitates and manages the process of evolution of a group of consciousnesses, including the planning and coordination of intraphysical lives during the intermissive period.

evolutionary duo – an intimate couple positively supporting each other in their evolutionary journey.

existential program – the unique life-task of an intraphysical consciousness, planned and agreed to in the previous inter-missive period, with the assistance of the evolutiologist. Designed to maximize the evolutionary opportunities of the current life. Not transferable!

extraphysical – relating to non-physical dimensions and consciousnesses manifesting without a physical body.

extraphysical office – the assistential energetic space, established through the prolonged practice of Penta, that allows advanced extraphysical helpers to provide direct assistance to unwell intra- and extraphysical consciousnesses close to the physical dimension.

frontochakra – the chakra located at our forehead, in the area between our eyebrows. Also known as the 'third-eye' chakra.

groupkarma (group + karma) – karma generated with regard to the group of consciousnesses with whom we are going through successive periods of intraphysical and extraphysical existences. Often used to refer to family, friends and colleagues. See also egokarma and polykarma.

helper – an extraphysical consciousness of above average evolutionary intelligence and discernment, dedicated to assisting others in their evolution.

holosoma (holo + soma) – the complete set of somas or bodies that the consciousness uses to manifest in different dimensions. All the vehicles of manifestation of the consciousness together. For an intraphysical consciousness the holosoma is made up of the soma or physical body, the energosoma, the psychosoma and the mentalsoma.

holothosene (holo + thosene) – the set of thosenes or thoughts, sentiments and energies generated by one or more consciousnesses over time. A holothosene is the energetic fingerprint of an individual. The holothosene of a place is defined by the dominant thosenes produced there by both intra- and extraphysical consciousnesses over time.

Homo Sapiens Serenissimus – a consciousness that is fully aware of only needing to complete one or a few more physical lifetimes to end its evolutionary cycle in the physical dimension. Enjoys a state of profound and imperturbable serenity that harmonizes every dimension where it manifests.

immanent energy – primary energy, impersonal and neutral, dispersed across the entire universe. Also known as *Chi*, *Prana*, zero point energy.

intermissive period – the period between two physical lives during which we manifest in the psychosoma in extraphysical dimensions.

intraphysical – relating to the physical dimension and consciousnesses manifesting with a physical body or soma.

intrusion – see consciential intrusion

mentalsoma – the body of discernment, the most subtle body of the consciousness used to manifest in the mental dimension.

morphothosene (morpho + thosene) – subtle energetic forms created through an individual's thosenes. In the extraphysical dimension these forms can interfere with a projector's perceptions and assume objective reality.

multiexistentiality – the multitude of physical existences or lifetimes experienced by a consciousness.

Penta – acronym for Personal Energetic Task, a daily practice in which the intraphysical consciousness spends between 40 and 60 minutes emitting therapeutic energy for the benefit of intra- and extraphysical consciousnesses, acting in the capacity of mini-piece to an extraphysical team of helpers.

polykarma (poly + karma) – karma generated by a consciousness through profoundly ethical actions for the benefit of consciousnesses at large, driven by a sense of fraternity with all, free from bias relating to any superficial traits of manifestation such as gender, race, religion, politics or even species.

precognition – mental and sensory impressions of events to come in the future.

projectiology – the science that studies the projection of consciousness, or the out-of-body experience, and the projection of bioenergies beyond the holosoma. A subdiscipline of conscientiology.

projection of consciousness – the action in which an intraphysical consciousness temporarily leaves its physical body of manifestation in another, more subtle, body to manifest in extraphysical dimensions. Also known as astral travel, out-of-body experience, soul travel.

psychosoma (*psyche* + soma) – extraphysical body of manifestation of the consciousness. Synonyms: astral body, emotional body, spirit body, spirit double.

resoma (reactivation + soma) – the reactivation of a new physical body or soma after an intermissive period. Commonly referred to as 'conception' or 'birth'.

retrocognition – a memory relating to a previous life.

self-mimicry – see consciential self-mimicry.

sympathetic assimilation – the deliberate installation of a close energetic connection with one or more consciousnesses leading to an assimilation of the other person's energies for therapeutic purposes. Sometimes this enables the person who installed the sympathetic assimilation to decode aspects of the thosenes of the other person(s).

sympathetic deassimilation – deliberate cessation of a sympathetic assimilation, often by applying the energetic technique of the vibrational state.

thosene (THOught + SENtiment + Energy) – a compound term to capture the fact that thoughts and sentiments (or emotions) always come together and produce energy. Each thosene represents a unit of manifestation of the consciousness producing it.

transcommunication – the use of electronic devices, such as tape recorders, radios and computers, as mediums for communication between extraphysical and intraphysical consciousnesses.

Appendix

Learning More

If you have read the whole book, you will know that there are many things that can contribute to our evolution. A lot of these are the things life throws at us or, perhaps better, the parts of life at which we throw ourselves! They include our relationships and the challenges we take on, and they cannot be gained from books or courses. Still, there is a lot of benefit to engaging in some sort of more directed ongoing learning process. Once you start looking into and experiencing multidimensionality, you realize that the learning simply never stops.

While there are many systems that can help us to broaden our multidimensional understanding and self-awareness, for me conscientiology has now represented the benchmark for the past 16 years. What appeals to me is the breadth and depth of the analytical processes that aim to give us an understanding of ourselves as consciousnesses, beyond all the biological, psychological, mental and even extraphysical processes that might otherwise become our focus. As someone who is academically minded, I also enjoy the clarity of language, which allows for rigorous intellectual engagement, and I feel confident that this intellectual approach will eventually lead to an integration of conscientiology with the conventional natural and social science disciplines. If you have an interest in the phenomena and understandings described in this book, I highly recommend that you read some of the more technical textbooks and pursue the educational programs offered by conscientiology. Whatever else you do or whatever your framework, a basic background in conscientiology will enrich your knowledge and provide a deeper way of understanding your multidimensional life.

Further Reading

There are innumerable books on multidimensionality, many of which have provided me with helpful insights over the years. The ones that I have identified here were the standouts. They were books that really helped me to understand various aspects both of myself and the nature of consciousness. I also include a couple of recent introductory books on conscientiology. I have grouped them here according to the main topics they cover.

Introductions to conscientiology

Gustus, Sandie. 2011. *Less Incomplete: A guide to experiencing the human condition beyond the physical body*. Alresford: O-Books.

Minero, Luis. 2012. *Demystifying the Out-of-Body Experience: A practical manual for exploration and personal evolution*. Woodbury: Llewellyn.

Vieira, Waldo. 1999. *Our Evolution*. Rio de Janeiro: International Institute of Projectiology and Conscientiology.

Projections of consciousness

Buhlmann, William. 1996. *Adventures Beyond the Body: How to experience out-of-body travel*. New York: HarperOne.

Monroe, Robert. 1971. *Journeys Out of the Body*. New York: Doubleday.

Vieira, Waldo. 1997. *Projections of the Consciousness: A diary of out-of-body experiences*. Rio de Janeiro: International Academy of Consciousness.

Vieira, Waldo. 2002. *Projectiology: A panorama of experiences of the consciousness outside the human body*. Rio de Janeiro: International Institute of Projectiology and Conscientiology.

Ziewe, Jurgen. 2008. *Multidimensional Man: An authentic eyewitness account of the world that awaits us after death*.

The significance of retrocognitions

Alegretti, Wagner. 2004. *Retrocognitions: An investigation into memories of past lives and the periods between lives*. Miami: International Academy of Consciousness.

The (conventional) science of multidimensionality

Tart, Charles. 2009. *The End of Materialism: How evidence of the paranormal is bringing science and spirit together*. Oakland: New Harbinger Publications.

The International Academy of Consciousness & The Center for Higher Studies of Conscientiology

The International Academy of Consciousness (IAC) is a not-for-profit organization dedicated to the development and teaching of conscientiology across the world. The IAC was originally founded in October 2000 with the aim of constructing Europe's first conscientiological research campus. Then, in May 2002, the scope of the organization expanded when all of the IIPC offices outside of Brazil were transferred to IAC, including its research, educational programs, human resources and scientific publications. The IAC thus inherited the experience and accomplishments of the IIPC team, which had worked internationally since 1994.

Since its formation the IAC has hosted a number of large events at its research campus near Évora in Portugal, including the First Symposium on Conscientiological Research in October 2005, the Global Symposium on Existential Inversion in November 2006, the Second Symposium on Conscientiological Research in October 2008, and the VI Consciential Health Meeting and IV Symposium on Self-Conscientiotherapy in October 2010.

It has also performed several large research experiments, and its instructors have developed 81 original courses on topics within conscientiology (as of December 2010). The IAC's courses emphasize the practical experience of multidimensionality and parapsychism, with the following two being salient examples:

The Projective Field, a three-day immersion course for inducing lucid out-of-body experiences; and Goal: Intrusionlessness, a one-year course that focuses on developing parapsychism and freedom from intrusion. Below are the contact details for the IAC's main offices in different countries.

In addition, there are many different organizations in Brazil that teach conscientiology. The global hub of the discipline is the Center for Higher Studies of Conscientiology in Iguassu Falls, Brazil. Waldo Vieira presently resides there, and the center has attracted hundreds of researchers from across Brazil and beyond who are developing new teaching techniques and increasing our understanding of the multidimensional manifestation of consciousness. Just like our IAC offices and our own IAC campus in Portugal, the campus in Iguassu Falls welcomes visitors and researchers from around the world. You can find more information about the Center for Higher Studies of Conscientiology on its website: **www.ceaec.org**

Here are the contact details for IAC offices around the world. If you don't find one near you, send an email to the one closest to you or check the website, as courses are offered in many other towns and countries from time to time: **www.iacworld.org**

Contact details for IAC offices

Australia
Email: australia@iacworld.org

Brazil
Email: brazil@iacworld.org

Cyprus
Email: cyprus@iacworld.org

Finland
Email: suomi@iacworld.org

France
Email: france@iacworld.org

Germany
Email: germany@iacworld.org

Italy
Emails: bergamo@iacworld.org or milano@iacworld.org

Mexico
Email: mexico@iacworld.org

Netherlands
Email: netherlands@iacworld.org

New Zealand
Email: newzealand@iacworld.org

Portugal
IAC Research Campus
Phone: +351 (26) 895 91 48
Herdade da Marmeleira EN 18, km 236
Évoramonte, Estremoz
Email: campus@iacworld.org
Other cities
Emails: lisbon@iacworld.org; porto@iacworld.org

Romania
Email: romania@iacworld.org

Spain
Emails: barcelona@iacworld.org
madrid@iacworld.org
seville@iacworld.org

Sweden
Email: sweden@iacworld.org

Switzerland
Email: geneva@iacworld.org

United Kingdom
Email: london@iacworld.org

United States
Emails: arizona@iacworld.org
austin@iacworld.org
boston@iacworld.org
california@iacworld.org
florida@iacworld.org
newyork@iacworld.org

About the Author

Kim McCaul is a consultant anthropologist in the areas of Australian Aboriginal land rights, heritage and cross-cultural awareness. He has a long-standing interest in cross-cultural conceptions of consciousness and multidimensional life and has published a number of articles on these topics. In 1995, he started researching his own consciousness through a visit to a meditation center in Indonesia, and since 1997, he has been using the theoretical and practical frameworks of conscientiology to increase his multidimensional understanding. He is currently a volunteer with the International Academy of Consciousness (IAC), an organization dedicated to developing and teaching conscientiology, and has given talks and workshops in Australia, Brazil, England and Germany. He runs regular IAC workshops in Adelaide, Australia, where he lives with his wife and three children.

You can find more information about the multidimensional understanding discussed in this book and connect with Kim through his website www.multidimensionalevolution.com

BOOKS

6th Books investigates the paranormal, supernatural, explainable or unexplainable. Titles cover everything included within parapsychology: how to, lifestyles, beliefs, myths, theories and memoir.